THE CREDO SERIES

VOLUMES ALREADY PUBLISHED

RENÉ DUBOS
THE TORCH OF LIFE

R. M. MAC IVER
THE CHALLENGE OF THE PASSING YEARS

F. S. C. NORTHROP
MAN, NATURE AND GOD

MOSES HADAS
OLD WINE, NEW BOTTLES

ERICH FROMM
BEYOND THE CHAINS OF ILLUSION

WILLIAM O. DOUGLAS
THE ANATOMY OF LIBERTY

HANS KOHN
LIVING IN A WORLD REVOLUTION

JAMES BRYANT CONANT
TWO MODES OF THOUGHT

POPE PAUL VI
DIALOGUES

FRED HOYLE
ENCOUNTER WITH THE FUTURE

THE CREDO SERIES

PLANNED AND EDITED BY
RUTH NANDA ANSHEN

DIALOGUE WITH MYSELF

BY

MARTIN C. D'ARCY, S. J.

A TRIDENT PRESS BOOK
NEW YORK 1966

Prepared under the supervision of
POCKET BOOKS, INC.

LIBRARY OF CONGRESS CATALOG NUMBER: 66-15723
PUBLISHED SIMULTANEOUSLY IN THE UNITED STATES AND CANADA
BY TRIDENT PRESS
MANUFACTURED IN THE UNITED STATES OF AMERICA

Ventatem Facientes in Caritate
"Living the truth in love"

St. Paul: Letter to Ephesians
Ch. 4.v.15

The Motto of Campion Hall, Oxford University

Dedicated
To the Master and Members of
Campion Hall, Oxford University
Past and Present

CONTENTS

THE CREDO SERIES

Its Meaning and Function

The Credo Series suggests that an epoch has come to an end, an epoch in which our best knowledge has been dimmed with boredom or darkened by destruction. We have felt for too long that this must be the very nature of life; this is the way life is, and to such a degree that life has consented to shrink from its own terrors, leading us to a deep apostasy of the heart and a crucifixion of our natural aspiration for experience and growth.

The absolute has surrendered to the relative. Our era of relativity, however, whether in science or in morals, does not allow us to assume that relativity implies an absence of ground to stand on, and therefore a relaxation of all effort toward foundations. "There is no firm ground," the dominant malaise of our time, this acceptance of non-finality, summons us to a heightened task. For the failure of formulated absolutes leaves the absolute requirement to evaluate again that uncaptured reality which contains and guides the total meaning of our existence.

The Credo Series hopes to unlock a consciousness that at first sight may seem to be remote but is proved on acquaintance to be surprisingly immediate since it shows the need to reconcile the life of action with the life of contemplation, practice with principle, thought with feeling, knowledge with being, and work, no longer a form of punishment as in the Judaeo-Christian tradition, but accepted as a way toward the growth and realization of the self in all its plenitude. For the whole meaning of self lies within the observer and its shadow is cast naturally on the object observed. The fragmentation of man from his work, the being of man into an eternal and temporal half, results in an estrangement of man from his creative source, from his fellows and from himself.

The symbol of *The Credo Series* is the Eye of Osiris. It is the inner Eye. Man sees in two ways: with his physical eyes, in an empirical sensing or *seeing* by direct observation, and also by an indirect envisaging. He possesses in addition to his two sensing eyes a single, image-making, spiritual and intellectual Eye. And it is the *in-sight* of this inner Eye that purifies and makes sacred our understanding of the nature of things; for that which was shut fast has been opened by the command of the inner Eye. And we become aware that to believe is to see.

Thus, it is suggested, there may be born a sharpened vision, which comes from seeing reality as the incarnation of associations and affinities with something beyond the visible self. For it is our hope to show the human relevance of ideas, the ways in which knowledge can help us to live in the immediate and real world by pointing to the confluence of man and his vocation, of subject and object, by reverencing the curious and mysterious metabolism between man and matter, the sacred nexus between the person and his work, and by asking whether the freedom now released through the creative energies of mankind will bring salvation or destruction, the answer to which will depend upon the aims we cherish.

The Credo Series submits that the universe itself is a vast entity where man will be lost if it does not converge in the person; for material forces or energies, or impersonal ideals, or scientifically objectified learning are meaningless without their relevance for human life and their power to disclose, even in the dark tendencies of man's nature, a law transcending man's arbitrariness.

For the personal is a far higher category than the abstract universal. Personality itself is an emotional, not an intellectual, experience, and the greatest achievement of knowledge is to combine the personal within a larger unity, just as in the higher stages of development the parts that make up the whole acquire greater and greater independence and individuality within the context of the whole. Reality itself is the harmony which gives to the component particulars of a thing the equilibrium of the whole. And while physical observations are ordered with direct reference to the experimental conditions, we have in sensate experience to do with separate observations whose correlation can only be indicated by their belonging to the wholeness of mind.

It is our endeavor to show that man has reached a turning point in consciousness, that his relationship with his creative self demands a clarification that can widen and deepen his understanding of the nature of reality. Work is made for man, not man for work. This Series hopes to demonstrate the sacramental character of work which is more easily achieved when the principal objects of our attention have taken on a symbolic form that is generally recognized and accepted: in other words, when there is an established iconography relating to the meaningful interpretation of man and his vocation. This suggests a "law" in the relationship of a person and his chosen discipline: that it is valuable only when the spiritual, the creative, life is strong enough to insist on some expression through symbols. For no work can be based on material, technological or physical aspirations alone.

The human race is now entering upon a new phase of evolutionary progress, a phase in which, impelled by the forces of evolution itself, it must converge upon itself and convert itself into one single human organism dominated by a reconciliation of knowing and being in their inner unity and destined to make a qualitative leap into a higher form of consciousness that would transcend and complement individual consciousness as we know it, or otherwise destroy itself. For the entire universe is one vast field, potential for incarnation, and achieving incandescence here and there of reason and spirit. What to some is mystery and inscrutability, to others symbolizes and declares the very nature of the cosmic process. And in the whole world of *quality* with which category by the nature of our minds we necessarily make contact, we here and there apprehend pre-eminent value. This can be achieved only if we recognize that we are unable to focus our attention on the particulars of a whole without diminishing our comprehension of the whole, and of course, conversely, we can focus on the whole only by diminishing our comprehension of the particulars which constitute the whole.

This Series is designed to present a kind of intellectual autobiography of each author, to portray the nature and meaning of the creative process for the creator and to show the relevance of his work to the feelings and aspirations of the man of flesh and bone. This Series endeavors to reflect also the influence of the work on the man and on society and to a point to the freedom, or lack of freedom, to choose and pursue one profession rather than another. It attempts to emphasize that the creator in any realm must surrender himself to a passionate pursuit of the hidden meaning of his labors, guided by deep personal intimations of an as yet undiscovered reality.

These volumes endeavor to indicate that it is impossible to know what constitutes a good society unless we know what defines a good individual. The self is determined by the values according to which it subordinates and integrates the rest of its values. If the values be transient, so is the self. If the values be dispersed and incoherent, so is the self. If they are organic and integrated, so is the self. The unity of human personality is its soundness. The unified self cannot be understood in terms of its constituent parts as dissected away from each other. So that finally what we see and what we do are no more and no less than what we are.

It is the effort of *The Credo Series* to define the new reality in which the estrangement of man and his work, resulting in the self-estrangement in man's existence, is overcome. This new reality is born through the reconciliation of what a man *knows* with what a man *is*. Being itself in all its presuppositions and implications can only be understood through the totality, through wholeness. St. Paul, who, like Isaiah before him, went into the market place not to secularize truth but to proclaim it, taught man that the "new creation" could be explained only by conquering the daemonic cleavages, the destructive split, in soul and cosmos. And that fragmentation always destroys a unity, produces a tearing away from the source and thereby creates disunity and isolation. The fruit can never be separated from the tree. The Tree of Life can never be disjoined from the Tree of Knowledge for both have *one and the same* root. And if man allows himself to fall into isolation, if he seeks to maintain a self segregated from the totality of which he is a necessary part, if he chooses to remain asunder, unrelated to the original context of all created things in which he too has his place—including his own labors—then this act of apostasy bears fruit in the demiurgical presumption of *magic,* a form of animism in which man seeks an authority of the self, placing himself above the law of the universe by attempting to separate the inseparable. He thus creates an unreal world of false contexts after having destroyed or deserted the real. And in this way the method of analysis, of scientific objectivity, which is good and necessary in its right place, is endowed with a destructive power when it is allowed to usurp a place for which it is not fitted.

The naturalist principle that man is the measure of all things has been shattered more than ever in our own age by the question, "What is the measure of man?" Post-modern man is more profoundly perplexed about the nature of man than his ancestors were. He is on the verge of spiritual and moral insanity. He does not know who he is. And having lost the sense of who and what he is, he fails to grasp the meaning of his fellow man, of his vocation and of the nature and purpose of knowledge itself. For what is not understood cannot be known. And it is this cognitive faculty which is frequently abrogated by the "scientific" theory of knowledge, a theory that refuses to recognize the existence of comprehensive entities as distinct from their particulars. The central act of knowing is indeed that form of comprehension which is never absent from any process of knowing and is finally its ultimate sanction.

Science itself acknowledges as real a host of entities

that cannot be described completely in materialistic or mechanistic terms, and it is this transcendence out of the domain of science into a region from which science itself can be appraised that *The Credo Series* hopes to expose. For the essence of the ebb and flow of experience, of sensations, the richness of the immediacy of directly apprehended knowledge, the metaphysical substance of what assails our being, is the very act itself of sensation and affection and therefore must escape the net of rational analysis, yet is intimately related to every cognitive act. It is this increasing intellectual climate that is calling into birth once more the compelling Socratic questions, "What is the purpose of life, the meaning of work?" "What is man?" Plato himself could give us only an indirect answer: "Man is declared to be that creature who is constantly in search of himself, a creature who at every moment of his existence must examine and scrutinize the conditions of his existence. He is a being in search of meaning."

Theory and life always go together. An organic conception of man and his work, man and society, man and the universe, is portrayed in First Corinthians 12 when Paul relates the famous story of the strife that once broke out between the parts of the human body. They refused to fulfill their special functions within the organism until they finally learned that they are all parts of one body and can exist and function only as such. For they all breathe together. And by so doing subordinate themselves to the presentation of the whole body. What may be an explanation of organic life in the human body may be transferred to the life in the universe and to the relationship between the interior and the exterior, for all is permeated by the life-giving creative power—by unity.

The authors in this endeavor are aware that man in the

twentieth century finds himself in the greatest revolution since the discovery of agriculture. They show, each in his own way, that part of the meaning of our present turmoil may indeed lie in its being the means to reconcile thought and action, to overcome the parochialism of dogmas that only isolate man from man and man from the implicit meaning of his chosen profession. Our effort is to create an image of man intelligible and unitary, a microcosmic mirror of the greater macrocosm of which he is a part and in which he has his legitimate place in relation to the whole. For even the extraordinary successes of scientific predictions, the fruits of man's ingenuity in inventing the scientific method, seem comprehensive only on the basis that the human mind possesses an inherent logic closely parallel with the structure of the external world itself.

The very interdependence of the observer and the participant can no longer be ignored as part of the essential value of things. To take a definitive example from modern cosmology, it is challenging indeed to note that there is a most unusual connection between the existence of stars and the laws that govern the atomic nuclei. Emphasis is placed upon the existence, not the properties, of stars. For everyone expects the properties of stars and atomic nuclei to be related. It is the *connection* with the *existence* of stars that is so reassuring—and indeed surprising.

From this it is evident that there is present in the universe a *law* applicable to all nature including man and his work. Life itself then is seen to be a creative process elaborating and maintaining *order* out of the randomness of matter, endlessly generating new and unexpected structures and properties by building up associations that qualitatively transcend their constituent parts. This is not to diminish the importance of "scientific objectivity." It is, however, to say that the mind possesses a quality that cannot be isolated or known exclusively in the sense of objective knowledge. For it consists in that elusive humanity in us, our self, that knows. It is that inarticulate awareness that includes and *comprehends* all we know. It consists in the irreducible active voice of man and is recognized only in other things, only when the circle of consciousness closes around its universe of events.

The experience of the modern mind has been expressed in terms of conflict produced by false dualisms, disruption, self-destruction, meaninglessness, purposelessness and desperation. This character of our time has found its expression in literature, in art, in existential philosophy, in some forms of natural science, in political demonologies, and is explored in the psychology of the unconscious. Our authors hope to indicate that through a quickening of awareness man can overcome this dualism and can rise to face the meaning of life and work, keeping his mind and energies awake at full stretch. Such knowledge—that form of knowledge which cannot be disjoined from being—will enable man to embrace life with passion and to work with devotion. It will enable him to absorb experience with his whole nature and thereby to fill a want that is satisfied neither by action alone nor by thought alone. This unity of *being* and *doing* has a justifiable claim to be called a form of enchantment since through it men, who might otherwise give in to the malice of circumstances and conditions, find their old powers revived or new powers stirring within them, and through these life is sustained, renewed and fulfilled.

Man is now confronting himself with the compelling

need to create an organic identification between what he *is* and what he *does*. For only in this way can the threat of conformism and the treachery of abstraction, the plight of the modern mind, be conquered. This split, inherited from the seventeenth century, between the transitive and the intransitive, between the creator and process of creativity, has blunted man's appetite for experience. Language itself in our time has failed because man has forgotten that it is the mother of thought, because of its analytical emphasis, and thus lacks ready means to convey associations, emotional or imaginative, that cluster around a subject and give to it a distinctive personal significance. In other words, the symbols by which man lives and has his being, that "tacit coefficient"* of articulate knowledge that is unanalyzable, now knocks at the portals of consciousness waiting to be admitted. For human nature loses its most precious quality when it is robbed of its sense of things beyond, unexplored and yet insistent.

The Credo Series belongs to those ideas that are intuitively conceived and that originate in spheres of a spiritual order and surprise thought, as it were, compelling it to transform its inherited notions conformably with its enlarged vision of the nature of things. It is as though the authors of the Series were recovering this reality out of a memory of a lost harmony, a memory latent in the soul and not distilled from the changing things of mere physical observation. In this way the inner unity of the known and the knower may be preserved, and the almost mythic intuition of reality thereby related to its conceptual and rational forms of expression. For man, unlike a machine,

* See the classical work, *Personal Knowledge,* by Michael Polanyi for an enlarged meaning of the nature of reality. (Chicago University Press, 1958.)

is an organism existing as an end in itself. He *is* the system on which causal explanations are based and to which they have to return; he *is* a historically existent whole, a four-dimensional entity, and not merely an abstraction from which statements about phenomena are deducible under the guise of eternity.

Our hope is to point to a new dimension of morality—not that of constraint and prohibition but a morality that lies as a fountainhead within the human soul, a morality of aspiration to spiritual experience. It suggests that necessity is laid upon us to infer entities that are not observed and are not observable. For an unseen universe is necessary to explain the seen. The flux is seen, but to account for its structure and its nature we infer particles of various kinds to serve as the vertices of the changing patterns, placing less emphasis on the isolated units and more on the structure and nature of relations. The process of knowing involves an immaterial becoming, an immaterial identification, and finally, knowledge itself is seen to be a dependent variable of immateriality. And somewhere along this spiritual pilgrimage man's pure observation is relinquished and gives way to the deeper experience of awe, for there can be no explanation of a phenomenon by searching for its origin but only by discerning its immanent law—this quality of transcendence that abides even in matter itself.

The present situation in the world and the vast accretion of knowledge have produced a serious anxiety, which may be overcome by re-evaluating the character, kinship, logic and operation of man in relation to his work. For work implies goals and intimately affects the person performing the work. Therefore the correlation and relatedness of ideas, facts and values that are in perpetual interplay could emerge from these volumes as they point to the inner synthesis and organic unity of man and his labors. For though no labor alone can enrich the person, no enrichment can be achieved without absorbing and intense labor. We then experience a unity of faith, labor and grace which prepares the mind for receiving a truth from sources over which it has no control. This is especially true since the great challenge of our age arises out of man's inventions in relation to his life.

Thus *The Credo Series* seeks to encourage the perfection not only of man's works but also and above all the fulfillment of himself as a person. And so we now are summoned to consider not only man in the process of development as a human subject but also his influence on the object of his investigation and creation. Observation alone is interference. The naïve view that we can observe any system and predict its behavior without altering it by the very act of observation was an unjustified extrapolation from Newton's *Celestial Mechanics*. We can observe the moon or even a satellite and predict its behavior without appreciably interfering with it, but we cannot do this with an amoeba, far less with a man and still less with a society of men. It is the heart of the question of the nature of work itself. If we regard our labors as a process of shaping or forming, then the fruits of our labors play the part of a mold by which we ourselves are shaped. And this means, in the preservation of the identity of the knower and the known, that cognition and generation, that is, creation, though in different spheres, are nevertheless alike.

It is hoped that the influence of such a Series may help to overcome the serious bifurcation of function and meaning and may show that the extraordinary crisis through which the world is passing can be fruitfully met by recognizing that knowledge has not been completely dehumanized and has not totally degenerated into a mere notebook over-crowded with formulas that few are able to understand or apply.

For mankind is now engaged in composing a new theme. Life refuses to be embalmed alive. Life cannot abjure life; nothing that lives is born out of nothingness. But nothing, either, can preserve its form against the ceaseless flux of being. Life never manifests itself in negative terms. And our hope lies in drawing from every category of work a conviction that non-material values can be discovered in positive, affirmative, visible things. The estrangement between the temporal and non-temporal man is coming to an end, community is inviting communion and a vision of the human condition more worthy of man is engendered, connecting ever more closely the creative mind with the currents of spiritual energy which breaks for us the bonds of habit and keeps us in touch with the permanence of being in all its plenitude through our work.

And as, long ago, the Bearers of Bread were succeeded by the Bearers of Torches, so now, in the immediacies of life, it is the image of man and his vocation that can rekindle the high passion of humanity in its quest for light. Refusing to divorce work from life or love from knowledge, it is action, it is passion that enhances our being.

We live in an expanding universe and also in the moral infinite of that other universe, the universe of man. And along the whole stretched arc of this universe we may see that extreme limit of complicity where reality seems to shape itself within the work man has chosen for his realization. Work then becomes not only a way of knowledge, it becomes even more a way of life—of life in its totality. For the last end of every maker is himself.

"And the places that have been desolate for ages shall be built in thee: thou shalt raise up the foundations of generation and generation; and thou shalt be called the repairer of the fences, turning the paths into rest."*

* Isaiah, 58:12

—Ruth Nanda Anshen

DIALOGUE WITH MYSELF

MY CREED

A creed is a personal belief and can stand for both a personal invocation and a philosophy of life. It is as a philosophy of life that I have expounded my creed, my *credo,* in the pages which follow. Moreover, I have tried to show this development of my ideas through my reading and the influence of great teachers upon me. What they have to say is at least interesting, even when a reader may disagree with their views. I use therefore a form of dialogue, with others as well as with myself, in place of controversy which is in keeping, I hope, with the ecumenical spirit now prevailing—seeking and sifting, that is, rather than objecting and contradicting.

Thought which is admired and loved becomes part of one's being, and so it is at times difficult to separate one's own ideas from those one has lived with for many years. I have been lucky in the friends and teachers I have met and I here express my lasting gratitude to them.

I am especially grateful to Ned O'Gorman for useful criticism and for enlivening my manuscript.

M. C. D'Arcy, S. J.

INTRODUCTION: ADMISSIONS FREE

Theology used to be the queen of the sciences and its influence permeated all education. Faith is a cosmic attitude, a kind of Italian sunlight in which, as the fogs and mists fade slowly away, human nature stands out more clearly with its distinct virtues and faults. History takes on a new sense and hope in man is restored. If a human being be a special image of God and so dear to God that God was prepared to take on the form of a man and suffer on a cross for love of him, this dearness cannot be exaggerated and he must not be subordinated to any larger whole, be it state or system, which thwarts or nullifies his grandeur. (God's love is not a quantity and is given fully to each without loss to God or to others.)

In this respect the Christian belief differs wholly from the Marxist. Communism looks to the future, to a time when, with the withering away of the State, a classless society will emerge. At the end of this forward movement of man, they say, there will be a millennium; injustice and strife will cease, and each will give according to his powers and receive according to his needs. The past cannot share in this happy time; they are already dead—stone-dead. Their one consolation in this lifetime is to have been the manure for the harvest. My Christian view, on the other hand, is that every generation can call itself blessed in that it is God's intention that every individual should enjoy a happiness far surpassing that of the classless society. It is the person and the community of persons who are most worth considering.

Let me, then, stay for a time on some of the questions and problems which arise regarding persons. This is not so easy and congenial a task as it appears for, strangely enough, educators, statesmen, and thinkers turn away from persons and spend their time considering them as concepts and abstractions. It was Martin Buber who made us realize how often we think of others as things, using an I-it relationship and not an I-Thou. The living God has been variously described as a cosmos, Whole or Absolute, an ocean of being, or even as a bung hole without a barrel. In education a marvelous system can be devised, but if it have a poor teacher it goes in one ear of the pupil and out the other. A good teacher on the other hand can mold the young no matter what he teaches. This shows the power of personality and also its dangers. A witch doctor and a fanatic both can play on their audience and create a following. Nowadays a close study is being made of methods of brainwashing and conditioning of the mind. (I have heard it said by the ill-informed or by enemies of the Catholic Church that members of the Society of Jesus are so conditioned as to be like sticks in the hands of their superiors. They ignore the fact that the Exercises of St. Ignatius of Loyola, which are the instrument of this conditioning, start with purely rational considerations. It is only after reason is satisfied that the appeal is made to love and self-sacrifice in imitation of Christ.)

Most, I am sure, would agree that in their lives it was persons who had a transforming effect on them. When I was young, I owed a great debt to a man with an outstanding personality and power over students. Later, he was to have the same magnetic effect on aristocrats, boxers, stevedores, police, and doctors. My commonplace standards in scholarship and criticism were shown up, and I was drawn by him to delight in beautiful things and to seek the almost unattainably high. Later, when I was wrapped up in philosophy and art, it was a priest who showed me by example what love of one's neighbor could achieve. Almost more influential was a boy I had been sent to teach. He was the youngest son of Augustus John, the painter, by his first marriage. He had something of the boisterous and wayward genius of his father, but his gift lay in writing and speaking, not in painting. He looked like a handsome gypsy, and he grew so spontaneously by his own original insights that I hesitated to give him conventional learning lest it should adulterate his strangely individual genius. He was one of the few who, I thought, would lose and not gain by going to universities such as Oxford or Cambridge. In the end, Oxford philosophy did dry him up for a while and interfere with his own singular outpourings in poetry and in prose. He had an earthy humor and joy and yet, like an ancient god, the earth could not hold him. He would prefer a tree to a hotel for a bed at night, to curl up in it like an animal after days of unbounded energy, then start off on a new adventure in the morning and give away all his money before his first stop. If my memory be right, friends of his father like T.S. Eliot and Wyndham Lewis, felt that he was unlike all others in his youthful genius. His death by drowning in Cornwall nearly broke his father's heart. To one like myself, babbling literature and delighting in dialectic, he was a breath of fresh air bidding me not to live at second-hand on books, not to read about colors and nature, but to enjoy nature, to enjoy knowledge. Above all I felt with him the presence of a fellow human being, a presence I know he could transmit to a parson or a peasant, to an Arab in the desert or an Indian on the banks of the Amazon. He had become a Catholic as a boy, and his faith was like a campfire round which the young laughed, men sang and worked, and cows jumped over the moon.

It would seem as though in becoming civilized, we usually have to lose in order to gain. A native has an overcharged sensory apparatus, and as his mind grows, his sight and hearing and smell lose in power. I used to wonder when I was young why the learned were so often neither wise nor human and their values so wrong-headed. Nietzsche wrote contemptuously of the philosophers who "sit on the steps in the shade out of the rays of the sun knitting the trousers of the spirit." D. H. Lawrence also reacted strongly against Bernard Shaw and the anemic intellectuals he met. This reaction can go too far with sneers at good manners and human civilized habits, but it can, I saw also, prepare the way for the iron crook of the Communists and the iron shod boots of the Nazis. True culture has to combine a love of life and a love of truth, as well as find room for various kinds of human living, for the adventurous Captain Cook and Lindbergh, for a Colonel Lawrence and a Teilhard de Chardin and a Churchill, as well as the scholars of the Sorbonne, Oxford, and Harvard, and Nobel prize winners.

Another lesson I learned from persons occurred when I was a young priest. I was sent for a few weeks to look after a slum in the parish of a large city. I started off filled with the idea that loving-kindness would be the open sesame to the hearts of my parishioners. They were a fine, rough, independent set of people living in miserable conditions. At one of my first encounters a rather fierce looking woman looked me up and down, and then said disparagingly that the priest whose place I was taking was a real priest, a real man of God. If the people were not on time for church on Sundays, she told me, he would come with his stick, get them up and out, and march them to church. These words, and this attitude, were to me a revelation. I saw that my loving-kindness seemed to many of these people to be a weakness. They did not like this milk-and-watery love. It was then I understood for the first time why God behaved as he did in the early stories of the Bible. God is love, but love has often to be translated; its blaze has to be accommodated to the mentality of the recipient. If Yahweh had spoken the language of Christ saying, "Come to me for I am meek and humble of heart," the still half-savage people of Israel would have turned to the cult of Baal, seeking revenge on their enemies. They would have no truck with what would seem to them womanish *faiblesse*. Even today we have the problem in Africa that the intransigeance of Islam is more attractive to many than the Beatitudes of the Gospels. Love, therefore, needs a preparation before it can be accepted for what it is. Never, perhaps, will it be properly understood without the supporting virtues of justice and mercy. Once I saw how God must shrink his blaze to shine in the weak, childish eyes of early humanity, and how even now there is a constant increase of understanding as the ages pass, I felt that certain religious and theological difficulties came into focus. The Greek Orthodox theologians have a word "economy" to elucidate the relation of God and man, and His treatment of man. It is a difficult doctrine, for it can easily look like a defense of lying or compromise. Perhaps we are better suited now to understand it. Centuries ago everything important was thought of as fixed and static. The natural law was like a stone dropped from Heaven, and time and growth of knowledge could make no difference in our understanding of it. But now we see that time enters into scientific theories, and man, swaying about in a kind of dialectic and disturbed by new crises and conditions, is ever renewing his knowledge, purifying it and seeing better into essential meanings. This has happened in connection with the gospel teaching. We hold the same doctrines as the Apostles, but we do not have to fight the battles they did over foods pagan and unclean, and circumcision, nor do we expect the second coming any day. The early Christians took some time also to understand that Christ's good news was not for any particular race or time, but for the whole world. I might say that almost up to the calling of the Ecumenical Council, old bigotries persisted, and it was all too easy to label those who did not belong visibly to the Church of God as outside God's loving providence and as God's enemies. Now we are beginning to see God's handiwork everywhere in the vast panorama of history, and we announce with joy that Christ's saving work is retrospective, as well as forward-looking.

In the Bible the mysterious figure of Melchisedech stands as the symbol of God's loving agency amongst the unknown peoples of the world. Their aspirations and forms of worship bring them to the steps of the temple. They attend upon Christianity, which is the model and visible expression of God's mind and will. Christ caps all desires. He is the dénouement of God, for he is "the image of the Invisible God." "All things have been created through and unto him, and he is before all creatures, and in him all things hold together." In Christ we learn what God is like, and therefore we have to take as finally true that God is like a father who has unceasing care of all men without exception, and this care is such that he counts even the hairs of our head. We are told expressly by Christ's beloved disciple that God is love, and it follows from this that there are no limits to what God is prepared to do for all men born into this world.

This truth is disguised and hidden from us by the emphasis in many Christian prayers on sin and its deserved punishments. Here the justice of God is invoked in order that man should have a correct knowledge of himself and of the awe-inspiring perfection of God. This bears out what I have already written about the woman in the slum and her notion of love. The Church, conscious of its failures and sins, is ever asking for pardon. It is the better ones amongst us, those who have seen the heights, who are the first to appeal to God to forgive their gross abuse of liberty and man's chronic backsliding. But to balance this, I fall back upon the fundamental truth that God is love, and that outside all our puny reckonings His providence will work, and at the end His ways will not only be justified but adored. I can see clearly how the unique splendors of God's Word made flesh must stand out, an incomparable revelation of divine love and of the heights which man can attain by grace. Christian life—"I no longer live, for Christ lives in me"—is a new divine mode of living with God, and it is distinct from all purely human inventions, dreams, and ideals. This could not be otherwise, and any attempts to make a universal religion composed of choice bits from East and West must fail. I know that Aldous Huxley and Ananda K. Coomaraswamy have fallen for this idea. To me it is a pathetic and sometimes dangerous attempt to step outside our humanity, and I realized this vividly in an argument with Coomaraswamy. He accused me of sabotaging, in a book of mine, *The Mind and Heart of Love,* the great tradition of wisdom through the ages, a wisdom which is identical in all the highest religions, despite different passing forms due to the varying cultures in which they rose. This esoteric or higher wisdom is for the elect, not for the common multitudes, but it is the common multitudes whom a living God loves, and it is the unique character of the Christian faith to know the Word made flesh, a God in history, and an institution where mysticism and human art and common labor are all at home.

The Christian revelation as I see it gives us not only the authentic portrait of God; it also films for us man as he is and man as he changes through the generations. Even if, which God forbid, the image of God were faulty, the vision of man is so convincing that the Christian religion would taste like truth. Here is man, a being on the horizon of two worlds, the unearthly and the earthly, capable of startling holiness, gentleness, and self-sacrifice; a maker of lovely images, of ordered cities and systems of thought, and yet always so near to barbarism; unable to stay fixed to any one social or political ideal, divided in himself, brutal, avaricious, and hypocritical. Because he is like this he has desperate problems to settle in every age—world problems, city problems, and individual problems. History tells us of the wandering barbarian hordes who eventually destroyed the Roman Empire, of the brutal usages of slavery, of the divisions of castes, of the denial of human rights, and the almost equally disastrous plans of Communists, reformers, and secular liberals. The people stone the true prophets and bow down before the false; Christ is crucified and Socrates is sentenced to drink hemlock. The old saying about the necessity of eternal vigilance is as apposite now as in the days of Balthasar.

The Christian view of man rests half way between optimism about human nature and cynicism or despair. Some interpretations of original sin would have it that human nature is corrupt and capable of no good action without grace. How strongly I repudiate this! True, human nature has a bias to self-satisfaction, ease, greed, and concupiscence, but freedom is there to respond to what is good and God gave us a human nature of great warmth. I know that the Church in its anxiety for the weaker brethren at times plays the very cautious mother. Dismayed, for instance, at the Reformation, by the license and corruption, the Council of Trent put all Catholics to school—where discipline was strong. I remember, too, when I was young the after-effects of the Modernist heresy, and how carefully one had to tread. Many sighed under the restrictions. It must not, however, be forgotten that license unchecked can do untold harm and that the sufferings and myriad deaths of the Second World War could have been saved by a strong hand from the abuse of freedom. Libertarians, who look back to Rousseau and regard all restrictions on liberty as wrong, never see their mistakes until too late, whereas the Christian, with his deep sense of the importance of the human soul and the horror of sin, is inclined to impose too many rules.

P. Teilhard de Chardin saw in the progress of civilization the promise of a time when all mankind might be united in mind and heart. The growth of sovereign states in Africa and Asia is perhaps the most striking phenomenon of our day, and the attempt to capitalize it is seen in the institution of the United Nations. The various Christian bodies are also stirred by a hope of reunion. An ecumenical spirit is abroad; an amnesty has been declared, and former enemies are sitting together smoking the pipe of peace.

There remain among Christians serious conscientiously held differences of belief which will have to be resolved without any compromise of convictions. There is, too, as I see it, a larger problem. Can men develop without at least gentle disagreements and battles of wits? They have to be challenged to get the best out of them. This is a law of nature as the headings of evolution prove—the struggle for existence, the survival of the fittest, natural selection. In the case of human individuals and societies, resistances, oppositions, tensions have led to discoveries in science and medicine and new insights in the arts, in morals and politics and religious ideas. "The blood of martyrs is the seed of the Church," and it is almost as if a Lucifer were needed perpetually amongst us to change our slack and sleepy habits.

This kind of struggle or debate is now called "dialectic," a process of yes and no ending in a new synthesis or clarification. At present Christianity is faced with a formidable "No" from the secularist. The world can be lived in happily now and understood without appealing to the supernatural. A dialectic between science and religion is needed, therefore, even more than between science and the humanities. Here the words of the Dean of the Harvard School, Samuel H. Miller, are very much to the point. He is convinced that no second-rate or shopworn version of Christianity will do. "There is no way to share in the agony of our world, its darkness and shame and bewilderment, except by suffering what it suffers, carrying in our hearts what it carries in its heart and sweating through the Gethsemane of its travail and decision."

My own attitude, like that of Mr. Samuel H. Miller, is that it is better to take risks than to sit down and wait on events. For this, the moral ground must be firmly laid and such truths as the equality of all men take on a new life and actuality. I do not see, however, how a materialistic civilization can pay this truth and the truths of liberty and brotherhood any more than lip service. They are obvious only in the atmosphere of a spiritual philosophy, and indeed, in a specifically Christian one. Physical characteristics and empirical evidence provide no sure evidence for equality; the all-around man like Goethe or Lord Keynes is very different from a Mongoloid child; so too a member of the French Academy from a dweller in the Stone Age. We are only alike in possessing a soul made in the image of God and potentially free and responsible. In other respects the differences have to be taken into account, and it is here that a Christian philosophy of life is perhaps the only guarantee of a happy and peaceful future society. H. G. Wells described man as a prince in a slum. There is truth in this, but the prince can be an extortioner, and the slum-dweller an Oswald with a gun. There is a potential Abraham Lincoln and Adolph Eichmann in each of us. There are many influential writers and university teachers who shut their eyes to the facts and broadcast their illusions about human nature. The intelligentsia are slower than the Bourbons to learn from history. They love to use words like "sincerity" and "pure motives" and ignore the records of crimes in the newspapers, the sensationalism in popular literature, the scribblings on lavatory walls, the confessions in courts or on the couch of the psychiatrist. Now, to harp constantly on sin and negatives is merely exasperating, but a healthy optimism must include a dose of discipline and self-denial. The very struggle for existence calls for endurance and labor, and nowadays the hard conditions of the Middle Ages are paralleled by fierce competition in industry and the increasingly high demands made on students at universities and in schools of art and ballet. It is a pity that the same high standards are not extended to the training of the soul. The best in us so often lies hidden and needs the crisis or the call of love to bring it out. Even without the incentive of a spiritual ideal, the Soviet state has learned to respect the old rules of marriage and has changed the feckless, improvident Muzhiks into able mechanics, athletes, and scientists.

Winston Churchill has written that "civilization grows with morality and spirituality and expires without them. Mercy, pity, love, and peace." I would add "reverence" to serve as a guardian of the high mysteries amongst which our lives move. Marriage and family life, for instance, can touch the heights and they can serve our animal instincts. At present the question of birth control excites far-seeing statesmen, moralists, the ordinary citizen, and especially the Catholic. I had been brought up to believe that birth control by *coitus interruptus* or by the use of artificial means was morally indefensible. I understood that this was at bottom a moral matter and not a matter of Catholic dogma or discipline. It was on the same plane as lying or murder or sodomy. The Church, as the guardian of morals, had not the power of deciding on this matter, no more than it could ever justify murder. The arguments as given followed the traditional principles that misuse or abuse of a human function was wrong. For example, to drink too much was to abuse a function; to lie was to abuse the function of speech which should serve to share truth with others. I could see weaknesses in the arguments, but I had no trouble in accepting the doctrine because I felt the love relationship between a married man and a woman was intimately related to offspring—an act of creation and a taking part in a continuation of the race of man. Moreover, love could so easily descend to lust, and the sacredness and beauty of conjugal love would suffer.

Such was the view I took, one which had been generally accepted for centuries. But now Catholic thinkers have been called upon to reconsider traditional teaching on this matter, and they are now concerned to bring it up to date, the while the core of the Church's teaching is left intact. That teaching was based on what is called the Natural Moral Law—the primal dictates of reason, that is, with regard to conduct. The Church holds that it is powerless to change what is against nature, to excuse, for example, murder, lying or lechery. Contraception was taken to be like fornication or gluttony, an abuse of human nature in one of its most vital functions. This view went unquestioned in days when modern methods of birth-control were unknown, when population was scarce because of disease and war, and the length of life usually short.

But now the scene has changed, just as in reverse the question of the legitimacy of war has changed with the stockpiling of world-destructive bombs. Many urge that we now realize as never before the unique quality of a person, and with that the intrinsic goodness of marriage love both in itself and for maintaining the fair unity of family life. Of old it was assumed that the multiplying of the human race was a necessary duty, and so even bastards were half-tolerated. Now, on the other hand, the world as it seems will be so overpopulated that there will be no means to feed it, no way in fact in which human beings could live a proper life. The very good of society as a whole is therefore at stake, as well as that of family affection.

It would appear then that the problem should be debated on different terms, not exclusively on nature and progeny, but rather on wider and relevant issues hitherto unforeseen, and in the light of new moral responsibilities. Nature and natural law are still of ultimate importance in all these discussions and the Church which knows the weakness and strength of human nature cannot be rushed into new decisions. We all know from experience the example of the thin edge of the wedge, of how a relaxation in the marriage laws may bring the danger of promiscuity. If unproductive love be permitted on occasions, especially for hard cases, why should not agonized spinsters and homosexuals use the same argument?

Perhaps it is for these reasons that many hope as well as think that the problem will be resolved not so much by casuistry as by increased knowledge and control of the human body and its processes. Then marital love could be both beneficial and freely enjoyed without, as a distinguished physician has said, "the dismal application of a technique without grandeur."*

What I have been saying proceeds from a formed view I have of society and human relations. It is very unlike that of Hobbes, and it is neither stoic nor epicurean. Its basis for inspiration is the saying that "it is more blessed

* It may well be that soon a perfect apparatus will be invented, which will diagnose, with certainty, the "safe" periods.

to give than to receive." The motto of the college where I was brought up ran *Quant Je Puis,* Old French for "As much and as well as I can." I cannot say that I or many of my contemporaries lived up to this motto, for we were not especially hard-working. The text, however, which I have quoted is part of the heritage of Christendom, and the example of the founder of Christianity is always there to shock us out of self-complacency and self-regard. "Giving" in public life is put into practice in service, and so the respect and honor given to persons in society is graded by the nature of the service given to the community. In the Christian polity, the tradesmen were honorable in that the tailor clothed his neighbor, the butcher fed him, and the shoemaker shod him. Then in the professions the scholar was dedicated to wisdom in his degree of service and imparted it to others, the doctor spent himself on the health of the community, the lawyer stood for justice for all and protected the innocent, the priest looked after others' souls, the statesman worked for peace and the general welfare, the soldier was prepared to risk his life for his country. In the temporal order the king or ruler was at the top, power descending on him from God to rule according to law. Highest of all was the Pope because in this ideal of life, he was "the servant of the servants of God."

This scale of rank and honor may seem to belong to a simpler society than ours, but unless we fall back on a flat and unlivable form of equality, it can still serve as a corrective and an ideal. We cannot avoid distinctions—based sometimes on competence and at other times on monetary influence, but the calling in of a poet to read his work at the inauguration of a president reminds us of an age-long reverence for the poet and the seer. Institutions of education are multiplying everywhere, and there is the danger that they may become only stepping stones for careerism or centers for research, hardly distinguishable from the educational establishments now proliferating in Russia. In a race with the Russians on such terms, we might lose since they are single-minded, whereas we are vague in our aims and ideals. The spirit informing our civilization should be different from theirs, and the difference should be seen in the stress on the excellence of human freedom and the opportunity it gives for loving service. In a speech I made at a university commencement some years ago, I said that Dante gave us a lesson on how to grow wise. Our modern educators should learn from Dante in the face of a great confusion of ideas and ever-widening issues. We have to hold steadfastly to the nobility of reason and not surrender it to "those who have lost the blessing of high thought." We have "with wit and art" to lead the barbarian within and without us to where "hangs that sweet fruit . . . which will give to the hungry their peace." This was Dante's vision of wisdom. I should add to what I said then that as the world becomes one in science and economics, so it must also become one on a higher level by a better understanding of man and the joy of sharing. To quote another medieval poet: "love and lowliness and loyalty, these [should] be lords in the land, truth to save."

I

INTERPRETATION

THE CREDO SERIES proposes that a chosen group of scientists, philosophers, writers, and theologians should state not so much their views as the way their ideas came to take the shape they have and so form their personal credo. There are many Communists and Freudians, for example, and we tend to think that we know what such words stand for. We gain fresh insight into these systems when we follow a distinguished Marxian explaining to us how he came to turn to dialectical materialism and how it is relevant to contemporary life. Most of the contributors to this Series are, I expect, to some degree converts, in that they have moved away from the ideas they learned in youth and now have a new insight of their own. The changes may well be radical as in the cases of men like Nietzsche or Heidegger, Koestler or Aldous Huxley. I, on the other hand, have never had to begin all over again. I end where I began with certain beliefs, and these I have grown to enjoy more and more firmly and personally with the years.

The excitement of a revolution in outlook will not be there, nor again the experience of a pursuit of truth against the advice and approval of teachers and well-wishers. This might well be a handicap. Another handicap is this: the basic views I hold are well known, or supposedly well known; they have been expresed by innumerable writers in different countries. What is called "apologetics" forms a whole branch of religious writing, and many distinguished converts to the Catholic faith have written explaining and defending the choice they made. Now I conceive the purpose of this Credo Series to be different in that I am not obliged to give long arguments defending the positions I hold nor even to give a description of all the articles of my faith. I hope rather to present a view of life in a personal way; that is, as I see it and as it appeals to my understanding, with special reference to those who have influenced me.

A critic may, however, object that Catholics are not free to have their own view; they have to whistle to one tune. One must either say everything in unison or be a heretic. Moreover, what is believed is believed on authority and not on reasonable grounds. I must, therefore, begin with a vital distinction. I believe, in opposition to many Christians of other faiths, that reason has a vital part to play, first before the act of faith, and secondly within the faith as exploring and designing and recreating the contents of the faith according to one's personal vision. Faith may come as sunlight on the human situation, or at a certain point in reasoning, I reach the belief that Jesus Christ is without question the Word of God the Gospels claim he is. If he is the divine Word, then what he says is true, and it comes to me sealed and signed with divine authority. Christ is "the way, the truth, and the life," and as St. Peter said when others left Christ, complaining that his words were "hard sayings": "To whom shall we go? Thou hast the words of eternal life." But from then on, I am free to pursue with a new ardour the paths of truth opened up to me. My belief does not stifle my inquisitiveness; it excites it. One has only to look at the record of Christian theology to see this. The libraries of the pagans were from the beginning ransacked, and the discoveries of Plato and Aristotle were given a new setting. Between Augustine and a Gabriel Marcel or Teilhard de Chardin, there has been a heavenly music with many variations, and there is no reason why what is ancient should not be seen and heard as fresh in every generation. There has, in fact, seldom been a more profitable time than the present, when so much new knowledge in the various sciences has accumulated and needs to be worked into a new synthesis. A hundred years ago Lord Acton wrote that "there is an outward shell of variable opinions constantly forming round the inward core of irreversible dogma, by its contact with human science or philosophy, as a coating of oxide forms round a mass of metal, where it comes into contact with the shifting atmosphere." The metaphor here used it not altogether happy, but Acton uses it to express the truth that "the Church must always put itself in harmony with existing ideas and speak at each age in its own language." If it does not do this, the "true dogma is left in unnatural union with exploded opinion."

These very words of Acton have been quoted by a group of modern theologians who are discontented with the traditional attempts at synthesis by Christian theologians. They claim that the Christian religion needs a spring cleaning. The old vocabulary and the ancient, consecrated images are worn out; new attitudes and a new language are essential if Christianity is to survive. They do not fear to turn to current philosophies for help, even though these have been hostile or indifferent to the possibility of religious thought. It is well, perhaps, that I should make my own position clear as to my accord or disaccord with this new movement in theology before moving on. Its general outlook and manner of attack have been summarized by the Anglican Bishop of Woolwich, Dr. I. A. Robinson, in his *Honest to God.* Dr. Robinson says that the images and framework of the faith have been so tied to a prescientific mythology that they obscure it instead of serving to bring out its truth. He is especially irritated by the images of height: "he ascended into heaven," "the descent of the Holy Spirit," and all the talk about the "supranatural." Such language, he says, belongs to the pre-Copernican world consisting of a heaven above, an earth, and a hell below. He prefers the language of Paul Tillich who has written that "you must forget everything traditional that you have learned about God, perhaps even the name itself. For if you know that God means depth, you know much about him." Tillich also says that religion is "ultimate concern," and this is accepted by Robinson. Bultmann's views on "demythologising" and the *Letters and Papers from Prison* by Dietrich Bonhoeffer are also brought forward as illustrating the need of a radical change in our interpretation of Christianity. Bonhoeffer claimed that man has now grown up and no longer needs God as a child needs its father. We ought no longer to retreat from the ordinary way of thinking into a Christian ghetto of traditional formulae; the day of the supernatural is over, and God is to be found in the secular world in which we have to live.

This change of thought amongst Christian thinkers takes various forms, but there is a common denominator. Behind all is the Lutheran dislike of reason and the appeal to religious experience. No longer, however, is it considered safe to fall back upon something so uncertain and subjective as experience, for during the nineteenth century the liberal school of theologians by their criticisms of the Gospels removed the basis of such religious experience. In its place, however, something better, so it is thought, has come in. Kierkegaard blazed a new trail when, dismissing the enormities of German metaphysical thinking, he appealed to the naked condition and predicament of the individual self and introduced what is now called "existentialism." The language of the new writers to whom I have referred is full of expressions such as "self-involvement," "ultimate concern," "commitment," and the favorite word "blik." But there is something else, perhaps more formidable, in these new writers. They have taken under their wing the forces of modern positivism and they are using the new linguistic approach. That forces them to sacrifice much of the language of traditional theology to achieve what they desire. Some contemporary Christian thinkers deprecate any attempt to make a new synthesis or system. They rule out all such statements as "God exists," "God loves us," "God created the world," since they seem to believe, according to Mr. J. Heywood Thomas, "that a system of theology is doomed from the outset to failure." With such an assumption and when words have to be understood by their use and only retain meaning in this use, theological thinking and metaphysics receive short shrift. But whereas thirty years ago religious statements were called emotional noises, they are now being surreptitiously brought back under the guise of ethics and religious encounters. It is at this point that what the new theologians are saying may seem relevant. Having accepted the deposition of the royal intellect, they reinstate the name of God and of Christ through the voice of the people, challenging, wailing, and suffering.

If God cannot be verified in sensible experience, nor can a statement about God be contradicted, it follows that the word "God" is meaningless. Religion, therefore, cannot be accepted in terms of propositions which have to do with truth and falsehood. Donald Evans rescues the situation by recourse to the late Professor John L. Austin's linguistic distinctions. Austin has called one kind of statement "performative language." Religious language is not merely propositional; it is primarily a self-involving activity. God does not provide supernatural information about Himself; He addresses man in an event or deed which commits him to man. Man in turn commits himself to God. For him to know God is to acknowledge his divine actions, which themselves are performative or expressive. Such a return "performance" by man may lead on to acquaintance and an encounter with God. Aware that in thus describing the relation between God and man he may seem to be assuming some preceding knowledge of God, Evans insists that the "acknowledgment" resembles what happens in an aesthetic experience, when the act, the experience, and the illumination are simultaneous. This illumination is not, however, knowledge of which truth or falsehood could be predicated. He will not allow that we know God in this way even in our encounter with Jesus Christ. It is in the deeds and events of the Bible that we are first interested and we then take up an attitude and what he calls an "onlook." Whereas the Thomist philosopher would say that we can acquire some knowledge, however inadequate, of God by analogies, Evans trusts to parables: parables, for example, of the "potter" or of the "breath of life" or of the "Prodigal Son." When we read these parables, we feel that an attitude on our part is appropriate. I proceed to act as if I believed that there is a God who is like a potter. This is not just pretense or make-believe because I do take up a position in life and involve myself wholly. To put it in Evans' own kind of language: When God creates man, the performative force of His word overcomes the threat of meaninglessness represented by the Biblical image of sea and darkness. This gives a way of looking at one's own existence as in a parable. I see God protecting me from the chaos of a meaningless life. I adopt an attitude and I understand it in so far as I live in accordance with it, and thus grow in relation with God.

A grave weakness in contemporary explanations and expressions of faith is the absence of what really makes up true religion, namely awe and worship. God is reduced to being a factor and a language-word in the struggle for man's better existence. He gives man a pointer as to how to make the best of this world, how to be engaged in it and self-committed. What is subsidiary in the Gospels is given the chief role. Again the attempt to build a faith without knowledge is a forlorn one. It is all very well for those with a hearty mind and a healthy common sense to skip all the problems of knowledge and to find in Christ not only the saviour but the word of life. But it is very doubtful whether such an act of faith could occur without there being at least some idea of what God means preceding it, and there are countless numbers of people who have wrestled with the thought of God without knowing anything about Christ and Christianity. I know myself certain persons who complain that God has, so to speak, forced the faith in the divinity of Christ and in the Church upon them. It is first of all their reason which compels them to believe against their wishes. There are others who claim that they have argued themselves into the Church step by step, pressed on, so far as they can tell, solely by cogent arguments. But quite apart from such cases, does not the long history of religion and theological speculation prove that man has somehow always been in touch with a transcendent reality, which he then tends to portray and color according to his loves and fears. The general opinion of anthropologists is that behind the cult of local and tribal gods there is one Maker and Lord of all who is dimly acknowledged. Mircea Eliade and others have argued from the evidence that in early civilizations all was sacred, and it was only in the course of time that man appropriated to himself something and some place which he could call his own and secular. Modern theologians will not allow that the word God has any meaning save in the reality of one historical man. So striking and commanding is He that followers of Him are driven to commit themselves and to try to transcend their own limitations and act divinely. But a God who so treated man would indeed be a strange God, if he ever existed. We are not left sure whether he really existed; but if he did, he would not be the divine being celebrated by ancient thinkers and saints as one all holy and all loving. The very idea of a God who created man out of love and, nevertheless, left man in the dark, despite having a mind which could know his creation; such an idea is surely repugnant. This is bad enough; but there is worse. Man is left to carry on with a so-called religion which, instead of worshiping the living and true God, uses God to make the best of oneself in this world. In certain passages one or two of these writers seem to say that we can transplant names and say "man" when we mean God, and "God" when we mean man. "I am the Lord; that is my name, and my glory will I not give to another, neither my praise to graven images." (Isaias 13, 8)

Such views as I have been summarizing do not leave one the liberty to produce a new system of theology nor to attempt any kind of synthesis; and the reason is that the place of the intellect in human affairs has been diminished. Where we are no longer sure of the existence of God or of the nature of the universe, we have perforce to get religion back in devious ways, by emphasizing, for instance, the human predicament or by finding uses of language which permit us to talk morally and religiously. But I have not spent time on this new theology in order to find fault with it. Its message seems to me to be one which, if transposed into a new key, is both informative and illuminating. Then the limitation imposed by the dogmas of empiricism and linguistic analysis can be overcome. The principle of verification does not, as a matter of fact, cover all that common sense and theory accept as genuine forms of knowing. The sun goes on shining, and can be inferred, though some are skeptical about its reality. So too we are not bound to tolerate the statement that the name "God" is meaningless on the principle that no fact can contradict the statement. There have been too many to my liking who have changed over from being believers in God to agnosticism, and they would be insulted to be told that they had behaved irrationally and had no facts or arguments to support their change. The presence of evil, the history of man and evolution, can be and have been used as battering rams against the citadel of religion, and often philosophers have attacked religion by keeping a close watch on the use of theological language. This is right and proper, for it has always been the custom of philosophers to ask what a writer or speaker means by the words he is using, but it is quite another kind of tactic to stake all on language usage. Usages in fact can be very confusing and need another criterion, and the ordinary man assumes that his words can be tested by their accordance with reality. Without some such presupposition, usage would be almost as helpless as a computer.

Nevertheless, if we restore the mind, what these theologians have been doing can appear of great value. They make known to us afresh how thought and desire can work together and turn to action, and how realization and concern are immanent in the act of self-involvement. What they have to say bears especially upon religious attitudes and "onlooks." Donald Evans uses the word "onlook" to cover what is more than an opinion. It is autobiographical; it involves a pledge; it is expressive of an intention to act. If, for instance, I look on God as my Father, I adopt the outlook of the parable (fatherhood) towards my whole life. For us to be able to do this with regard to the Christ of the Gospels, we have to share to some extent His mind and His life and become like-minded with Him. Then and only then, the force of God's word will bring our life out of meaningless chaos into what gives us sustenance and life more abundantly. Now, to use the language of Tillich, my "ultimate concern" has hit upon an answer that can and should be lived.

In a book called *The Nature of Belief* first published in 1931, I used the old terminology in analyzing the act of faith in the Christian religion. The assent of faith was like to that of the moral judgment in that both committed one to an action. The moral assent, however, was concerned with means to ends or to minor ends, constituents of our moral life. Faith, on the other hand, was concerned with ultimates. I took my life in my hands and committed it to Christ, the Son of God. This was not, however, in any way an irrational act, for my mind saw Christ as "the way, the truth, and the life," all three. The process preceding the assent was like what happens in all processes of understanding and appreciation. One reads Plato, for instance, and at first suspects that Socrates is just playing with words; then a sense of the seriousness of the discussion develops and appreciation grows. Some reach such a degree of acceptance as to call themselves Platonists. Now the language and message of Christ are, let us assume, divine, and that message contains the good news of eternal life, our ultimate concern. Our human understanding boggles at it, but with the help of grace we reach at length what St. Paul calls "the mind of Christ." Then it is we cry out: "To whom shall we go? Thou hast the words of eternal life." This analysis, as it seems to me, is not far removed from those I have just summarized. But I do what the modern philosophers abhor, namely, appeal to supernatural grace as that which enlightens the mind to see and sets the will to act, and I treat the act as falling within the category of knowledge. In so doing, I have in agreement with me, as I think, the vast majority of those in the past who have considered this form of assent and others kindred to it. A good word here is "mindful," for it "reminds" us that as human beings the mind is immanent in almost all we do. Happy in some respects is the fate of our pet dog which lies on the floor untroubled while we read in the papers of floods and famines, births and deaths, and of the fine imposed on X for not leading his dog on a leash. *"Heu lacrymae rerum"* is spared the animal creation, nor does it notice the kind of jacket its mistress is wearing nor the "ultimate concern" which is wearing her down.

One test of the presence of mind and reason is that we are prepared to give our reasons why we adopt views. They may not be the whole story, but they play an essential part. By a trick of history, reason or intellect has been reduced to only one of its functions. Descartes tried to exhibit it in its pure state, and he left an unfortunate legacy. It came more and more to be associated with mathematics and then with scientific knowledge. Within recent years, it has lost its wholeness altogether and is kept for the so-called platitudes of logic and mathematics and for the knowledge of facts which can be empirically verified. Hence the modern theologian is disbarred and when he approaches religious truths, which cannot be got at by the only accepted rational methods, he is forced to play with the anti-intellectual prejudices of the time and by a tour de force restore the Christian faith by these odd means. He has to start off by saying that he may be "mad nor' nor' east," though he still can tell the divine windhover from a crow. The mind, in fact, pervades the self like a perfume and makes its presence felt in all man's activities. It seeps through all that we do as sweat through the pores of the skin. Modern psychoanalysts are driven in desperation to make mind play its part even in the unconscious, for what else is the game of hide and seek which they tell us goes on there? Thoughts high and lowly of God, of spirits and immortality have haunted man from the beginning, and just as it has been said that the more one tries to expel nature, the more sure is it to return, so the idea of God reappears again and again to affront those who say the idea has no content. How much more genuinely human and universal is the cry of the chorus in the *Agamemnon* of Aeschylus, "O Zeus, whoever he be, if by such a name it be pleasing to him to be called," and they go on to say that no matter what past image of him was incorrect, nevertheless who so sings songs of triumph in his honor will do right, for "he is a god who leads mortals on the way to wisdom." Even the following lines of Yeats show what he thinks God should be like, but is not:

> The years like great black oxen tread the world,
> And God the herdsman goads them on,
> And I am broken by their passing feet.

This Credo of mine is modest in its ambitions. It demands only that the reader be willing to accept the possibility of a coherent view of life. Such a view seems to me more and more necessary as departments of philosophy and science multiply and coordination between them grows more difficult.

I have met men whose minds have become so departmentalized that they can be in their political views Communists and religiously of the Christian faith, atheists in the laboratory and theists on Sundays. Moreover, there are varieties of experiences of which we are certain, which do not seem to fit into any pattern and indeed are contradicted by our general attitude to life. To give some examples of what I mean by our everyday certainties: there is the red blood when I cut my finger, the hard stone on which I walk, there are all the varying perspectives of a motor car approaching; then, I am aware of my own body and of its relation with my spirit, the presence of others around me like myself; there is a vague contour of a world; I know many past events, that Napoleon and Wellington fought the battle of Waterloo; I have heard or read of many places and take for granted that Great Britain is an island. Then I am always making decisions about right and wrong, and I am asking myself questions as to whether the assistance I can give to another person will in the long run be to his moral benefit. All such certainties and all such questions and decisions rest, as we suppose, on a solid world of truth, and it is disconcerting to find that general theories of the world and life abound which make nonsense of these certainties. Students are bound to read, some time or another, works of philosophers which conclude that human beings are not free or that they are just complicated pieces of machinery or domesticated animals, and that consequently the certainties of every day are without foundation. Some of these philosophers who hold such upsetting opinions do not seem to be at all disturbed themselves. I have seen an absolute idealist who did not believe in the reality of individual persons very annoyed by an importunate beggar, and a determinist marching in a procession to protest on behalf of liberty of thought. Lord (Bertrand) Russell must be almost an exception in realizing the inconsistency of his conduct and in being troubled by the problem. He has publicly stated that he has never been able to reconcile his passionate feeling that native peoples should not be maltreated with his general philosophy that morality is just an affair of one's private feelings.

I have sometimes asked myself to what extent I would believe myself bound to practice the virtues of justice and charity if I came to the conclusion that all human beings were no more than automata of a more complicated kind than a grandfather clock or a computer or a Rolls-Royce engine. A humanism without God or immortality, where there is no vindication of those wrongfully judged and punished, seems to me bad enough; but what of a real wasteland of a world where all moral ideals are only emotional noises? How reconcile the certainty of daily life that I must keep my promises and help the underdog and the accompanying knowledge that there is no foundation in reality for such certainties? Some might say that a certainty is a certainty and that one could argue from it that the general philosophy must be wrong or, on the contrary, that the certainty must go and that I can do as I like or perhaps that the certainty cannot be a certainty (strange as this may seem). Happy are they who can find an accord between their daily experience and their deliberately formed philosophy of life. For convenience sake I shall distinguish these two as the certain and the true. Our empiricists warn us of trying to find the true; it is a will-o'-the-wisp, they say. But in fact we both desire it and need it. We are, as the essayist has said, "in the odd position of living in an age of unprecedented scientific progress with nothing adequate to bring about its intellectual coordination." The existentialists realize the need for we are "plagued with all those pangs of conscience, innumerable as the flies of Argos" and the futility of life. Men turn to general views of life as they turn to the principal meal of the day. If it be not there as the meal should be, they invent one. And so it is that the general view, so far from supporting their daily experience, may undermine it. As a result a very odd result follows. In fact our certainties are bound to grow as experience confirms them. The sums we learned as children, the simple geometrical problems we solved, were certain from the first. Daily, however, evidence mounts up of their truth. Do our certainties increase with this new evidence? Or to put this in another way: does the child's knowledge of the multiplication table differ from that of a great mathematician or a great scientist like Einstein? If we are certain, how can we increase our certainty? May not the answer be that our first experience brings certainty and at the same time it forces us on to find a world to which it belongs, a world of knowledge, that is, based on reality? At any rate, what can with confidence be said is that behind and around all our direct experience is a vast universe which must be in accord with what we directly experience and, what is more, add or bring a note of universality to its truth.

By the truth I mean this order or system into which fits all we do and think. We all start off as one amongst others in a world; it rubs off our sharp edges, snaps back at us like a piece of elastic; and all our lives we are discovering what is new, getting rid of error and meeting its challenge. Some cannot face this challenge; others become too lazy. Normally, however, we try to make sense of this world of ours and to unify it into some kind of order. At first our ideas are those accepted by all around us, and it takes time to have an independent point of view, even in minor matters. Without being fully aware of what we are doing, we build up a set of opinions, composed of certainties, beliefs, and opinions. The vital question is whether they stand for reality, truly picture or represent or symbolize it, for only if this comes about can we enjoy the truth and be wise. Now while thinking on this subject and in process of writing a book upon it called *The Nature of Belief,* I was assisted by a suggestion in a manuscript written by Mr. H. Bickford. He laid great stress on what he called "the unity of indirect reference." What he meant was this, that one section of our beliefs is impressed upon us despite ourselves. Ordinarily we would split our beliefs up into those which nowadays are called platitudes, such as logical and mathematical truths, and truths which have been scientifically verified. As an alternative division, I give logical, metaphysical, and mathematical truths, truths of direct experience, sensible and intellectual, scientific truths, and historical and geographical data. Now Bickford pointed out that there are a number of truths which we would never dream of questioning. Though we do not ordinarily advert to them, our conversation and reading rely upon them and presuppose them. A simple, though not a primary example, would be the statement that Great Britain is an island. If I ask how it is that I am so certain of this, I find that the reasons I allege bear no relation to the certainty I possess. It is clear, for instance, that it does not depend on the number of times I have examined a map, nor the number of times it has been actually stated. Nor would the attempt to find out for certain by sailing round it avail for we might be sailing round an inland sea. Nevertheless our ancestors soon had no doubt about it. The reason is that all experience bore out the truth and there were so many indirect references to it that the truth fixed itself indelibly in our minds. Now this holds of all the most obvious truths. We rarely refer to them—and we would be dreadful bores if we did—but they are implied in our conversation and consultations all day long. They are primal truths which all experience vindicates. Within this class, it would be possible to make further distinctions, but that would be needless here. It suffices to say that many facts of history, such as the death of Queen Anne, the American Civil War, and again of geography, such as the existence of Tasmania and Siberia, are known in this indisputable way. Bickford called this certainty the "unity of indirect reference," and rightly so, because it is not as in science by multiplying the experimental evidence or by paying constant attention to what we are doing that the certainty is built up. Quite the reverse! Like the obvious, it is rarely referred to directly; we do however rely upon it indirectly in conversation, in reading, and when traveling. What happens is that the complexity of the evidence reaches such a strength that it strikes the mind by a compelling force of unity—a unity of infinite items which is richer and more intricate than any work of bronze hammered by a Vulcan into a pattern. Every moment winged words strike us, sensations leave their effects, and these hordes of impressions form into an order with a minute tracery like a thousand spiders' webs worked into one single web.

Here then is the most primitive and at the same time the most thorough and far-reaching way in which the mind makes contact with reality. The mind is to some extent passive; it is informed and molded by experience, and it is within this world of certainty that it begins its own personal interpretation of the world around. By supply and suggestion, it works upon us, and then we are waved on to do our own interpretation. Here is the marshaling yard where the mind gets its experience into order; for the mind is so constituted as to seek for unity and abide by a system which it feels to be true. How this works has been lucidly brought out by the late M. Merleau-Ponty in his *Phenomenology of Perception.* He criticizes the account given by the modern empiricist and intellectualist of how we come to pick up knowledge. The empiricist, he says, fails to see that we must already know for what we are looking; otherwise we should not be looking for it. The intellectual, on the other hand, does not realize that we have also to be in some way ignorant of the object of our search; otherwise we should not be searching. We are alert, therefore, to experience from the beginning; and what we do is to make something explicit and articulate out of what is presented to us as an indeterminate horizon. This follows, he says, from the fact, exposed by phenomenological analysis, that by our body we are already a part of the world in which we live. In this, man is like an animal which straightway knows which food is good for it. Our human acts, however, are distinct from those of an animal in that we can stand away from the encompassing reality, we can set it off at a distance from us and make it our inhabitation. To see, therefore, is to enter a universe of things which display themselves before us; to look at an object is to inhabit it, and from this inhabitation we go on to grasp all things in terms of that aspect which the things experienced present to us. For example, if I look at a bowl of flowers, I am not seeing only a color and a shape. I straightway attribute a table under it and a wall and a chimney to the room. As this is what actually happens, we must look upon our body which makes the world present to us as a kind of focal point of living meanings; it is not just the function of a certain number of variable terms. From childhood onwards, no matter how often we change our attitudes, we have one single world always on the horizon of our life, as the distant roar of a great city provides the background to everything we do in it. The image of the noise of a great city may be misleading, for whereas the noise is incidental, the world is not just incidental to our personal life. Merleau-Ponty means that we are bound up through our body with the world around us; it is within its unity that we are free to act and to grow.

I am, he tells us, an intersubjective field, not despite my body and historical situation; on the contrary, we are born of this world and in this world. For the same reason it is open to us with all its possibilities. Hence we do not merely accept the world; we choose it and give it a style and a significance.

In his lectures given at the National Gallery of Art in Washington, D.C., and later published as *Art and Illusion*, E. H. Gombrich develops this theme of interpretation. We take part far more than we think in our judgments not only of the artist but also of the child and the philosopher. He writes that the "true miracle of the language of art is not that it enables the artist to create the illusion of reality. It is that under the hands of a real master the image becomes translucent." In teaching us to see the visible word afresh, he gives us the illusion of looking into the invisible realms of the mind—if only we know, as Philostratus says, how to use our eyes. He takes the example of the painter Constable to show us how this power of interpretation develops. From Constable's notebooks we learn that all his art proceeded out of a child's loved landscape. "The sound of water escaping from mill dams, old, rotten planks, slimy posts, and brickwork, I love such things. . . . I shall never cease to paint such places; painting is with me another word for feeling, and I associate 'my careless boyhood' with all that lies on the banks of the river Stour; these made me a painter." So it was that a loved landscape became the scheme through which Constable saw his world. The schema enlarged itself so as to take in much else beside the banks of the Stour, yet those banks were strong enough to sustain a universe and see it fairly.

Even the artists sense their mind at work: Robert Frost wrote that " a poem begins in delight . . . it ends in a clarification of life, not necessarily a great clarification, such as sects and cults are founded on, but in a momentary stay against confusion." So ever green is the habit of mind that the very name of God can be dragged in and made to stand by a Chicago philosopher for "a system of cosmic patterns making for the maximum of mutuality." More people can reach up to God, I think, than to such "cosmic patterns," but it remains true that we are always trying to make sense of our experience. The child from the first is full of curiosity and tires its parents by always asking "why?" It takes its world from those about it in these first years, and then begins to make its own world, one at first too full of its own fancies, but harkening more and more to experience. Then comes the time when the child now grown up has to find its way in a world of conflicting ideas of every kind of subject from religion to dress. Usually, however, tradition exercises a strong hold upon the individual so that in many of their attitudes people from New York differ from those in Kuala Lumpur or Constantinople. Nevertheless on the greatest issues we are all "traveling to Byzantium" or choosing cities of the mind marked Scientific Materialism or Marxism or Lotus or Cyprus or Samarkand of the arts.

Exceptions, of course, appear to exist to this generalization. There are flibbertigibbets; there are others whose minds go to seed or are so cluttered up with miscellaneous knowledge or gossip that they do not seem to have any consistent personal view at all. Again, others appear to be numbed by some shock and withdraw as soon as a serious subject is introduced into conversation. Lastly there are the bovine sort, but more often than not, they are very deceptive and so they cannot be quoted against my generalization. Nor can those who profess themselves to be skeptical and take a pleasure in dissent be brought up as adverse witnesses. They protest too much and take sides so strongly that it is clear they have made a positive view out of a negative, like those who make a positive religion out of the worship of Nothingness. Most of us, anyway, are alike in making for ourselves a habitable universe in which to live, though the kind of hero chosen for imitation may be as different as Omar Khayyam and St. Simeon Stylites.

One last preliminary difficulty remains, and as I have already dealt with it in part when discussing Dr. Robinson's *Honest to God* I need not stay long on it. "Everything changes; nothing stays." Can beliefs remain unaffected by time? Now one of our certainties is that in human history there is always change; change of fashions, styles, and even of institutions. A Yankee could not easily live at the court of King Arthur. Homer's *Odyssey* and Joyce's *Ulysses* have the same theme, and they are far apart. Oxford and Cambridge have continued for seven hundred years, but what was taught in the thirteenth century has little connection with what is taught now. (Some may think this a loss.) On the other hand, many now would unite in singing the same Credo. We have then to accept enormous changes in all that touches our material life, and we have to report a development in humanitarianism in private and public relationships, in the application of a fixed morality in the law courts, and in the transition from credulity to strict methods of weighing evidence in historical and scientific investigations. Furthermore Dr. Robinson was rightly anxious that the truths of the Christian religion should be stated in a language which was intelligible and in accordance with modern knowledge. This means that there should be, as it has been remarked, an organic continuity between culture and, for example, the life of the artist and religious.

The answer to the objection that the Christian religion must fare like other cults and fade away in time is this. First there are always coordinates to cultures which do not change. Michael Polanyi has brought this out in his *Personal Knowledge*. Moreover, "looking back on the immensities of the past, we realize that all that we see there, throughout the universe, is shaped by what we now ultimately believe. We do know that the phylogenetic centers which formed our own primeval ancestry have now produced by a deployment which compared with the long ages of life on earth looks like a single sudden outburst—a life of the mind which claims to be guided by universal standards. By this act a prime cause emergent in time has directed itself at aims that are timeless." Within this category of timelessness, we look at the highest activities of the human mind. Its great works of art are timeless; likewise its conquests of nature, its philosophy of man, and its moral and religious ideals. It may be that these ideals and truths are of such a plenitude that we can take them in only by a dialectic in which one aspect has to be corrected by another, or it is just human waywardness which makes man wander to the sides instead of keeping to the middle of the road. What remains indisputable is the power of man to look before and after, to contemplate the nature of reality and to be mindful of his neighbor. With such talents, man is able to seek a view of the world that is at once coherent, possible, and joyous.

II

INSIGHTS

In the preceding chapter I have tried to clear the way for a Credo. Now I must make it clear that within my Credo there are all sorts of ideas to play with and to embrace. I saw, as every Catholic sees, staring me in the face, what I thought to be the expression of God's mind. But I had to learn to digest it, consciously or unconsciously, in my own way. Most of us, I suppose, who have had to lead a life of study would fancy that there were some important stages or crises in their thinking which revolutionized their outlook. Where the change was not total, it might be a matter of swapping ideas with another or exchanging systems as a Cartesian might turn over to Kant. But we each have, I discovered as I searched for my own Credo, an inner impulse or fate, a kind of Ariadne thread, that together with our free will, shows us the way to go. We each have our own inner impetus or fate, as we can discover when we look back. When we are old, we know exactly what we can do, and our reading is dictated by these specific and personal needs. In early manhood most of us read widely and might, as we think, have followed up various lines of thought. Gradually, ideas coalesce and take their individual shape and direction and become as distinctive as a highland tartan. In late years we may think we have new ideas, but if we look back on more youthful efforts we shall be surprised and rather ruffled to find these same ideas peeping out, even if they were only fledglings.

The series of ideas which have taken shape in my mind, giving flesh and blood to a Credo, I now see to have been immanent in what I thought from the beginning. Home and schooling gave them a certain cast, but I am not thinking of that. It was probably, as often happens, the gaps in my early education which first made my thinking personal. At the beginning of the century, my schooling followed the usual routine of the classics, mathematics, and a little science, with some history and English literature, mostly Shakespeare, worked into the curriculum. Religious teaching consisted of catechism explanations and apologetics. Felt, however, in the atmosphere was the old English Catholic tradition. The writers in it were sturdy and clear, though on a narrow gauge. Outside its teaching lay a wilderness, and within the fold, severity prevailed. The penal days had left their mark and the spirit of Jansenism had touched it. The revival of Thomism and the consequent new interest in philosophy and theology had only just begun to stir English Catholics. The chief personality of the time was Friedrich von Hügel, but he and others were under suspicion of Modernism. I was too young to be swept into that storm. I knew von Hügel in his later days and was greatly impressed by his spiritual genius, though I felt him to be a man of insights rather than a systematic thinker. Despite all the shocks to a sleepy orthodoxy, the general Catholic view did not seem to me to be affected. God was still in his heaven (despite Dr. Robinson), and all could be well in a world of good will.

The Christian view of life did provide a uniquely complete view of life, one in which every individual counted. Created by a living God; watched over by a loving Providence; possessed of free will with a world in which to win my spurs; offered the means of grace and the society of the new covenant, the Church of God; brought into union with Christ, God made man; presented with a vision of utter felicity, unless through one's own fault one lost one's soul; life for me had a purpose, and time seemed to be God's contrivance to allow me to grow and play my part in a vast drama.

This was the kind of unity I was taught, and the interpretation put upon it. The clinching truth, however, in all this pageant of ideas came in the knowledge of Jesus Christ. The Gospels have been subjected to a higher criticism; they have been pulled to pieces and demythologized; but all such attacks leave the mystery of Christ intact. Indeed, if some of the criticism be true, the mystery is increased. It seems to me that there is no figure in history comparable to the Christ of the Gospels, and if four different writers, different in their mental gifts and artistry have succeeded in making such a unique and consistent character, more than a miracle has taken place. He belongs to this world. He is at home in Bethany and Capharnaum, and yet He does not belong to this world. His language in the Sermon on the Mount and at the Last Supper is of a visitor, one who has come with a message, the bloodstained message of good news. The Gospel writers can narrate His fears and agonies and the most degraded form of death without lowering Him in our eyes. Far from that; He seems to grow in majesty in these records of Him; so much so that when the writer of the fourth gospel begins with the extraordinary statements of the Prologue that He was the Word of God and that in Him was life and that life was the light of man, we do not feel it odd or out of place or even exaggerated. In some ways the most remarkable sentence in the New Testament is: "And the Word was made flesh and came to dwell among us; and we had sight of his glory, glory such as belongs to the Father's only begotten son, full of grace and truth." Here is a declaration by one who had seen this man and perhaps had rested on his breast; and of this man he, a Jew acquainted with the doctrine of the Presence of God, the Glory or Shekinah (the word for "was made flesh" in the Greek is "eskenosen," "pitched his tent," with a play on the word "Shekinah") dared to say that he had sight of this Glory and spoken with the divine Word. Had not the truth of Christ's divinity impressed itself upon them so strongly, the Gospel writers could never have been able to give a consistent portrait of a man who could be both God and man at the same time. Let one detail suffice to bring this out: novelists and biographers have much greater difficulty in describing a good man than they do in describing a man in whom good and evil are mixed. In the case of Christ, the writers had not only goodness before them, but divinity as well. Now the good can so easily look condescending or too aloof or too single-hued to be described. The saints, the more perfect they become, the less do they attribute virtue or value to themselves. In their modesty their universal cry is as in the presence of a sinner: "There but for the grace of God go I." The figure in the Gospels, on the other hand, speaks with an absolute authority: "I say to you." He commands the sea to obey Him; He cures the sick and raises the dead and forgives sins, so the evangelists tell us, by His own authority, and we do not feel that assumption of authority is pride or madness, a kind of *folie de grandeur*.

Over thirty years ago now, I was one evening in a room with about a dozen other philosophers. It was on the occasion of an International Congress of Philosophy. The talk turned to religion, its nature, its forms and titles, its deeds and faith. After a time a philosopher from the north of Europe said that he had lost his Lutheran faith as a young man and been attracted to Leibniz and then to Kant and others. Finally out of curiosity he had gone back to the Gospels to pass a new judgment upon them. To his amazement, however, he realized after a time that it was not he who was the judge. He was himself being judged and by one whose standards were so absolute and final that he had to go on his knees. When he had finished, a Swiss philosopher proceeded to tell a story of himself with an identical ending, though he had had a different, Calvinistic, upbringing and had sworn by other philosophical masters.

If this be the impression made upon two thinkers by the Christ of the Gospels, and by impression I do not mean feelings so much as the light which accompanies the discovery of a truth, life will consist in seeing more and more of reality magnetized, as it were, like iron filings round this living truth. One could see that this happened to St. Paul and to the Apostolic writers. Taken together, the writings of the New Testament already present a theological unity so closely-knit, so living, and so novel that it seems beyond human construction. There have always been speculations about the nature of the spiritual world and what lies beyond our normal human experience. Mystics tell me of the one and the whole, of the transcendent and the super-essential. But Christ gives me the impression of being at home in these far-off spiritual regions. The heights of the spiritual life are so familiar to Him. He climbs the spiritual Himalayas, leading us on, as if the ascent were as well-known to him as a hill in Galilee. This is the decisive point of His revelation of Himself to the individual, for He makes clear to us the vision of holiness—and is in a sense Himself our holiness; and at the end of the vision is love laid bare more lovely than any human dream. The Pauline letters articulate the Gospels, acting like a fan, which, when it is opened up reveals what is hidden in the folds. St. Paul does more; he gives us the cosmic Christ against the setting of the powers of nature and the forces of the shining ranges of the firmament. He opens our eyes so that they are like to "eyelids of the morning." This vast universe, after the stories told of it by the astronomers, crushes us by its indifference as well as its size. The influence of the cosmic Christ is however so strong that we too become at home and we walk at ease and look with joy at the wonders of our God *(mirabila Dei Nostri)*. I said that Christ is himself in a sense our holiness. This is so because he is more to us than we are to ourselves; he is, too, within the self, in the "crypts" as the Gospel says, or depths, as a co-conscious worker, for, as it is written in lines attributed to King Alfred:

> To see Thee is the end and the beginning;
> Thou carriest me, and Thou dost go before.
> Thou art the journey and the journey's end.

I remember well the effect on me at school of the reading aloud of a poem by Richard Crashaw on the Nativity:

That the great angel-blinding light should
shrink its blaze to shine in a poor shepherd's eye,
That the unmeasured God so low should sink as
prisoner in a few rags to lie;
That Glory's self should serve our griefs and
fears, and free Eternity submit to years.

The music of the High Masses helped no doubt in those early years to make the Creed more and more a part of myself. Its articles were plain enough, though mysterious and couched in images which, as we have seen already, were of the kind to cause trouble in certain quarters. It was not so much the images as the theological form in which they were explained which proved unsatisfactory to my generation. It was a kind of trickle from the great systems of theology which flourished in the Middle Ages and in Spain and Flanders in the Counter-Reformation. The language was aridly scholastic, and little attention was paid to the fruits of scientific knowledge and the new methods of weighing history and the evolution of ideas. In the Middle Ages the truths of the Catholic faith had been treated systematically by original thinkers such as Aquinas and Bonaventure, Duns Scotus and others who even benefited by a healthy disagreement with each other. Logic-chopping and dry-as-dust thinking succeeded these great systems at the decline of the Middle Ages. Opposition to the views of the Reformers in the late sixteenth century gave a new lease of life to the old Scholasticism, but it grew to be too concerned with defense and criticism, and so it gradually declined. The Absolute Monarchs and the heirs of the French Revolution thought that they had attended its obsequies. This was not so, but Newman, who had a prophetic sense of what was to come and himself anticipated some of the more creative ideas of the morrow, was discouraged when he went to Rome after his conversion to find such poverty of theological thinking there. Later in the century at the instigation of Pope Leo XIII, interest in Thomism revived and gradually spread to the theological centers of Europe. England was to some extent isolated from this and other Catholic movements. Books, however, crossed the Channel, and the one which first inspired me was *L'Intellectualisme de St. Thomas* by Pierre Rousselot, a genius who was unfortunately killed during the First World War. In textbooks and in the schoolroom, thought meant reason —that is, syllogistic reasoning. There was nothing to do but argue laboriously to a conclusion. To Rousselot, intellect was the very life of the soul, a living activity, better than Bergson's élan vital, and by no means exhausted in the process of reasoning. The mind grasped the objects of reality and translated them into its own life in the form of concepts. In intuition the self saw itself in the very act of making an object its own; that is, it would be aware of reality, aware of itself, and aware of God its maker, all in one. This would constitute perfect happiness. In the process towards this epiphany, love is the dynamo. Intellect and love work together in a reciprocal relationship, love being a blind beggar and intellect a cripple with good sight sitting on the shoulders of love.

This metaphysic of knowledge was worked out by Rousselot with learning and acumen, but I have put it in more poetic form since Rousselot's metaphysic warmed the mind without answering all its questions. The death of Rousselot left his work unfinished, and it was more an hors d'oeuvre than a complete meal. So unexciting had been the scholasticism taught, and so scrappy, that for a short while I played with the idea of working on a Christian form of Hegelianism. In the later half of the nineteenth century, Hegel had become a favorite among English and Scottish philosophers.* My holiday with Hegel, however, came to an end when an admired scientific friend of mine said to me with some scorn that a philosophy should not be a toy to play with but a system to be lived. This remark has always stuck like a burr and its truth was more than verified thirty years later, when Existentialism was publicized and I read of Kierkegaard's remark à propos of the Hegelian system; that the world history of Hegel is of no interest unless one has a life of one's own, and, again, that there was no room in it for a sneeze. Nevertheless, such was the clinging attraction of Hegel that I needed the searching analysis of the Oxford realists to get it out of my system. Just in one matter, it had a lasting effect. In Hegelianism the individual and the community are organically connected, and the individual lives in the life of the larger whole. This larger whole is the life of the Spirit embodied. In such a system it seemed to me that the interests and autonomy of the self were not sufficiently safeguarded; but a real problem remained as to how to conceive of a unity in which the self would be related most intimately to others and to God and yet preserve its own personality.

The real reward of Oxford at the time was a heightened love of truth. The school of realists, of which Cook Wilson was the head, would have the truth and nothing but the truth, cost what it might. I had the privilege of sitting for hours and hours in a garden at Cook Wilson's bedside.

---

* The Olympian prose of William Wallace, now little quoted or read, entranced the mind, even as Ruskin's *Modern Painters* transferred a child's fairyland to a real world of beauty.

During his lifetime he was greatly esteemed, though he wrote very little. Cook Wilson held ordinary beliefs with extraordinary precision; he believed in God, in a free self, and in immortality. He reduced problems to their essentials and, like the mystic who at the end could say nothing but "God," tended to say that knowledge is knowledge, right is right, and goodness is goodness. Listeners did not realize how much cutting and cleaning and purifying had gone into the utterance of these triumphant platitudes. I was so pleased with these crystal clear statements that it took me a long time to realize that I wanted to say something more.

III

LIVING THE TRUTH

My Oxford studies made me certain that the intellect was a sure passport to reality. There could be no denying the mind's claims; it does not make the object; it apprehends it. This gave me certitude, but it did not help me much with discovering the nature of truth. My training was a hindrance for it lacked that sympathetic understanding which is so imperative if I were to make, in my mind, a kind of ecumenical peace among my philosophers and philosophies and arrive at a full, satisfactory system and view of life.

My interests at the time were philosophical, and it was only with time that they became more theological. Rousselot had provided a key which could open doors in his theory of how knowledge and love can be combined. Rousselot had leaned on St. Augustine; so it was natural to turn to him. Augustine had been an ardent Neoplatonist and he imbibed from them the idea of love as an attraction for, and an assimilation to, the highest. When he became a Christian, he found it easy to combine love and knowledge, for to him God was not only the paradigm of truth but also of goodness. The truths of this life were but shadows or images of His perfection, and the mind took satisfaction in looking upon God *modico ictu cordis,* "with a gentle stirring of the heart," and seeing all as dependent upon him. By a kind of Platonic dialectic, he passed upwards from creatures to the Creator, who in making them assigned to them their truth. Again, God was and is the one object who is supremely lovable, and He draws all to Him, as Aristotle said, by desire. Aristotle's God, however, had no interest outside himself and was not the Christian God Augustine had fallen in love with. Even the Platonists saw truth only "from afar off." The Christian God is the initiator of our human loves, for it is through God's antecedent love that we rise up to love him back. "I would not be searching for you if I had not already found you"; in this view Pascal and Augustine were at one. Knowledge and love, therefore, went hand in hand when it came to loving God. "Think you that wisdom is other than truth, in which the supreme good is beheld and possessed?" "The happy life consists of joy in truth; for this is a joying in Thee, who art the Truth, O God, health of my countenance, my God." Holding such a view, he was able to describe love as a kind of bias of the soul—"my weight is my love"—towards living truth. Where our heart is, there is our treasure, and a secret love within us dictates to us where to look and what to find.

Now this is all very well, and there are to my mind unforgettable insights in these meditations of Augustine; but how was I to reconcile them with the pure beam of knowledge requisite for truth in Cook Wilson's view? That in our ordinary thinking the subjective element plays a great part is certain. We have already seen some of the evidence for this in the excerpts from Merleau-Ponty and Gombrich. Opinions are usually colored by our likes and dislikes, and if knowledge too is subjective and biased, are we not, at best, halfhearted realists, like Kant, or purely subjective? We may not be able to deny the principle of contradiction or identity or some mathematical formula or the statistics given by a computer, but for the rest we are foredoomed to be capitalists or Communists, royalists or republicans, for city or for country life, image worshipers or iconoclasts, optimists who see everything through rose-tinted glasses or pessimists like Jacques who can suck melancholy out of anything as a weasel sucks eggs. Here was a difficult subject which I had to get right.

The fact that many a first-class thinker, philosopher, logician, or scientist can frequently fail to understand writings outside his subject shows that there is some other activity besides that of pure reasoning or knowing which is needed for understanding. It is strange that this has not been fully recognized by writers on epistemology. Perhaps they felt that they should leave the matter to the psychologists. In all human relations, to know is not enough; we have to share to some extent the thoughts of others, to enter into their minds and often to go behind their words to see the intention in what they are saying. There is no successful criticism in the arts until this is done and no advance in mutual understanding. A suitable description of this invaluable activity is *sympathetic understanding*. The difficulty, as I have said, is to make it square with the neutrality which is also supposed to be necessary in the sciences and in philosophical investigation. I attempted in a book called *The Nature of Belief* to show how the two worked together in what I came to call "interpretation." But before explaining this, I would like to say a word about an earlier essay, the first fruits of my thinking and containing a cloudy sketch of what I hold to this day. It appeared in a book called *God and the Supernatural*, and I quote from it as representing the first stage of my philosophical Credo. I began with the theory of knowledge I had derived from Cook Wilson—that knowledge contains within itself its own criterion; to ask for further arbitration about it as useless as turning out the light in order to see what one looks like in the dark. This is not equivalent to saying that we enjoy perfect knowledge. Far from it. The shifts to which we are put, the deductions and inferences we have to make so laboriously show that there are limitations in our ordinary processes of thinking which do not belong to knowledge as such. We feel that the direct intuitions of sense ought to have their counterpart in thought, and at times the lightning-swift apprehensions of the mind give us an inkling of what the mind is capable of. I knew my intellect was clogged by the nature in which it is implanted. We have to put subjects and predicates together, and we are very much at the mercy of our bodily states, the fatigues of the brain, emotional tensions, prejudices, and unconscious pressures. We are hampered by not knowing ourselves fully. We come to know something about physical nature around us, but our knowledge of living animals is by interpretation. As to human beings, philosophy is always turning them into things or individuals of a species. Interpretation here is needed even more and has to be supplemented by the sharing of common interests, mutual understanding, and fellowship.

This weakness in our intellectual apparatus means that we can never expect to grasp the nature of God. Ordinary persons and mystics are at one in their experience of a "cloud of unknowing" when trying to think of God. That does not mean that God is unintelligible to us or completely out of sight. All the evidence points to man feeling so dependent on a Maker that he has tried in all sorts of ways to circumvent the obstacles in the way of knowing God. Some modern theologians abandon natural theology altogether and rest their belief in God on the event of the Gospels. But this is a backward step, for it means shutting the eyes to the impact of religion throughout the history of the world and to the common element of worship in innumerable cults. In the Jewish faith there is the clearest recognition of the God whose son Jesus Christ claimed to be. There is hardly a single tribal history which is not also a religious one. It was this fact which led me to develop a suggestion thrown out in conversation by Cook Wilson. "God," I wrote, "is not a discovery or property of any particular age, no more than the idea of parentage or goodness." May it not be, then, that just as the idea of parentage or goodness arose because men were aware in some manner of parents and good people, so too the presence of a certain reality instinctively filled men with awe and created the special attribute of "divine" as alone appropriate to that being? What has happened is that men have bent down in adoration before a Being who stirred this response. This Being could not be a system or form. He must be a Lord God ten thousand times greater than the world, and sacrifice, which is a constituent of almost all worship, implies the recognition of this supreme sovereignty. When we consider how irreducible this idea is and how different from any invention or unrealized ideal, may we not conclude that it is born of reality in as true a sense as the ideas of body and spirit and personality?

We can inquire more closely into the way in which we arrive at this knowledge and establish its truth. Perhaps the two go together, or it may be that we have a simple belief in God as we might have in angelic spirits and that there comes a time when we have to confirm the belief or give it up. Catholic philosophers have in the past concentrated on showing that the belief is well grounded. They put into syllogistic form what St. Paul wrote in the *Letter to the Romans* about the pagans amongst whom his converts lived. "The knowledge of God is clear to their minds; God himself has made it clear to them; from the foundations of the world, men have caught sight of His invisible nature, His eternal power, and His divineness, as they are known through His creatures." This argument was converted by St. Thomas Aquinas into the argument to the First Cause and from contingency to God's necessary being. Many do not care overmuch for this kind of reasoning; some saying that they already know God; others that the God reached in the conclusion is not the living God revealed in the Gospels; while others again are altogether skeptical of this kind of metaphysical approach. In St. Paul's account God makes Himself known as a living, loving God, and this does not come out clearly in the traditional argument, efficacious as it may be. Moreover, if God be God, His relation with the creature must be of a unique kind and this is hidden in the general category of cause. The manner in which we come to apprehend what in the divine nature is distinct from all other real objects can be detected as follows. In general we can say that our reactions are determined by the nature of the object we encounter. Thus we react differently when touching a stone and a lizard. Shaking hands, again, differs from the touch of a lizard. In the world which we human beings share, we distinguish between the emotions caused by a new discovery, what we felt when we first heard of Hitler's concentration camps, and what most feel when looking at the inland sea of Japan or at Michelangelo's Creation of Adam in the Sistine Chapel. Most of us, too, would allow that it is the difference in the object we behold which is responsible for our reactions, and that our reactions are proper to that object. By this I mean that something would be very wrong with us if we felt indignation at, say, Christ's forgiveness of St. Peter and joy at meeting Herod after the massacre of the Innocents. In each case it is something outside us which is responsible for the kind of reaction we experience. Now throughout human experience there is to be found another reaction which is quite distinctive and which should therefore be able to give us a glimpse of a kind of reality as specific in its way as what is living, true, moral, and beautiful. This I will call the worshipful. As I wrote in the essay: "It is because nature is beautiful that the onlooker is mastered by a wordless aesthetic emotion, and it is because there is Someone walking in his own creation that we fall down and adore, overcome by the sense of reverence and awe." Men and women from time immemorial have felt the mysterious character of nature, its secret, the other side of its being. This is what St. Augustine meant when he wrote that the authentic voice of nature says "we made it not ourselves, but He made us who abideth for ever." Many modern anthropologists write of the "sacred." The words which best describe the emotion are reverence and awe, and this reaction is followed by acts of adoration or worship and usually sacrifice. What this comes to is that there is something or someone which inspires awe, adoration, and worship, and what is worshiped thus is what we mean by "God."

By the time *The Nature of Belief* came to be written,

the outer rim of my personal Christian Credo had been more or less filled in. The study of St. Augustine and Aquinas and Duns Scotus and others, partly by their very differences, served to bring home to me both personal and contemporary problems. Both Rousselot and Maurice Blondel, whose *L'Action* had a great vogue in those days, had been influenced by St. Augustine, and through them I came to appreciate Newman as a thinker.

Newman has not been taken very seriously as a philosopher. This attitude has now changed, and he is linked with Augustine, Pascal, and Kierkegaard as the precursor of Christian existentialism. *The Grammar of Assent* is both personal and universal in its intent. It represented the way in which the living mind works and forms beliefs, and it also depicted the travail of Newman's soul (and, at that time, my soul) to ground faith in truth. He felt that the logicians and philosophers had not paid enough attention to the actual way the mind develops ideas of its own and shapes them into belief. He pointed out that our firmest beliefs did not rest on conscious inferential proofs. To make clear what really happens, he coined the expresion "illative sense." Now this "illative sense" seemed to me to be the intermediary I had been looking for. It could tie together agreeably the authentic realism of a Cook Wilson with the sympathetic understanding which I had come to regard as so important—the guest master at the feast of reason. A realism without it seemed atomic and dead, but with it, could not one be forced into subjective idealism? Instead of the words "illative sense," I chose "interpretation," and by giving a number of examples from all departments of experience, I tried to show that we could not get on at all in human intercourse without it. The Gestalt psychologists had already proved that in our sensible experience we begin with a number of data which we see in a unity or as a configuration. These psychologists were concerned with the experience of the senses, and they remained psychologists rather than philosophers. Now what was true of the senses was equally true of the action of the mind. We are always interpreting the faces we meet, the writings we read, the documents we unearth, the past we study, the apparently unrelated physical data lying before us. It is this ingrained habit which explains why there are such varieties of conflicting views on almost every topic, social, political, athletic and aesthetic, philosophical and religious, and how it is that the genius by a bold stroke can at times resolve problems which have vexed scholars for centuries.

Here then is a form of knowing which is not necessarily subjective, nor so prejudiced as to make us blind to the facts before us. We could not know others as we do, their ways and their differences, or the similarities and dissimilarities between Japanese culture and Scottish culture, French wit and English humor, without it. In all cases the mind must know what it is doing, as the surgeon's knowledge speeds and guides his sympathetic fingers in an operation. The evidence must be there, even though at times scientists and historians appear to run ahead of it. Interpretation is present in scientific experimentation, but it is most rewarding in human relationships: to understand, we must become like the other. A mother can recognize the child's steps outside the front door, and the lover, so it is said in the *Song of Songs,* can know his beloved from one hair of her head. This line of approach brings us, as we have already seen, to the proper analysis and to the justification of the act of faith in Christ. Two men might have stood near the foot of the Cross. One could say that here is an unlucky man, perhaps innocent, dying; the other would look up and see a God redeeming. This latter experience befell Thomas the Apostle. On seeing the wounded hands and feet of Christ, he said: "My lord and my God." With that, all his memories and past knowledge fell into shape. This is where the intellect confirms the interpretation of the evidence and catches it up into a unity. In the case of the Christian faith, it assembles the scattered ideas into a new order. It not only makes sense of our human experiences; it also opens a door into infinity. The description of the faith in the *Letter to the Hebrews* is now seen to be exact, for faith really is "the substance of things hoped for and the guarantee of things unseen."

The fact that the ideas I had been following up fitted in so exactly with this description in the Hebrews was an encouragement to further investigation. The Creed has been explained in every generation in the same fundamental sense, though in different languages and with different emphasis. The fullest intellectual statement of it is by Aquinas in his *Summas*. It was congenial for me to write a book on his philosophical system and to lay emphasis on its dynamic character. The quiet, almost colorless, writing hid the love which vitalized all his thought. According to St. Thomas, God freely creates a world of independent persons and a contingent nature. New light was thrown on the metaphysics of St. Thomas by Étienne Gilson and others through a fresh understanding of the part played by such ideas as "participation." As a system, Thomism is *sans pareil*; it combines a self-sufficient philosophy and a theology as wide in its references and implications as Christianity. As a summa of Catholic doctrine, it is like the post office of a capital city. All that goes into it will be directed to the correct address. St. Thomas himself, however, was modest enough to say that he was trying to make the most of what was known at the time concerning questions outside Revelation, and so he left room for new insights and for systematizing on other principles than his own. Moreover, each age is preoccupied with problems which inspire or impede it and, consequently, insensitive to others. The Middle Ages, for instance, knew far more about God than we do, but less about man or, shall I say, individual men and women. The philosophy of man rested either on the Platonic idea of spirit not at home in the body or on the Aristotelian theory of the species of "rational animal." Both had their difficulties. The medieval scholar knew very little about physiology or biology and the part played by, for example, the glands, the thalamus and hypothalamus, and other parts of the lower brain in stirring emotions. He knew of only a few races beyond the Mediterranean and nothing about the primitive peoples who stretch back in history thousands of years. Year by year we learn more about the senses and the relation of the body to our thinking and remembering. The old theory of the four humors has gone, and in its place is not only a complex science of our conscious states, but also a new world of the unconscious.

When Dietrich Bonhoeffer says that man has now grown up and religion must, therefore, be sought in this secular world of ours and not outside it, his very exaggeration brought out the truth that man now is almost pathologically interested in himself. He is gazing into the mirror; he is undergoing treatment on a couch; he is full of concern and *angst;* and this in addition to all the modern claims for rights and privileges and a general equality and fraternity. It looks then as if a system of philosophy today might well begin with the human person. Such an interest is contagious and at one time I had half a mind to write a book on psychology. There was this strange thing called the self mixed up in a bundle with others, and at the same time, as Kierkegaard remarked so poignantly, in a desperate isolation, living as it were in an igloo. Each being had his own singular fingerprints and, nevertheless, in order to live a human life, he had to enter into communication with others and share their lives. The question of sympathetic understanding fitted in here. Now already even amongst medieval views one was drawn to take sides. St. Thomas said the soul was the form of the body and that the body provided the distinguishing marks and the individuality. At issue with him on this was Duns Scotus. Fortunately for me, Duns Scotus had a modern backer, whose influence on me for other reasons was great. This was the poet Gerard Manley Hopkins. In his *Note Books* he writes at length on the subject of the self. In one of his letters, he describes the joy which seized him when he discovered Duns Scotus. Scotus thought that Aquinas had omitted the core of the self in making the soul the form of the body. There must be a special "thisness" or singularity in the makeup of every human being. This view was a godsend to Hopkins whose whole bent of mind was towards the particular or singular. Students of his poetry know what importance he placed on what he called "inscape" and "instress." His theory of inscape involved an idea not so far removed from that of "sympathetic understanding." He believed that everything had its individual side or mark, and if one gave it one's undivided attention and sympathy, this object would reveal its individual mark of being. Hence it was his custom to look at the petals of a flower or a mica flake with abiding care, heeding what it had to declare. His word "inscape" stood for the outward reflection of the inner nature of the thing, the sense data which gave one an insight into the thing. When he spoke of the design or pattern of an object, he meant more than a harmonious ordering of the parts; it was the external side of the intrinsic virtue or excellence, not necessarily beauty, of the thing. By "instress" he meant the energies, or activity, or in his own words, the "strain of being." In one place he says that it is the "energy of being by which all things are upheld and strive after existence. It is the power which actuates their inscape." In what some would call a more mystical than philosophical statement, Hopkins says that in this stress of being the divine instress, which keeps the finite being in existence, is communicated. Nature becomes news of God, for the objects around us "are charged with love, are charged with God, and if we know how to touch them, they give off sparks and take fire, yield drops and flow, ring and tell of Him."

On the strength of these views, Hopkins maintained that every Tom, Dick, and Harry has a life and existence of his own, and this existence shows itself in an exercise and freedom which are unique. Each person can call himself an "I" and address another person as a "Thou." Every human being starts off with its own "pitch" of being, which can also be called freedom of response. He calls this self "a bare self to which no nature has yet been added, which is not yet clothed in or overlaid with a nature, is indeed nothing, a zero, in the score or account of its existence, but as possible it is positive, like a positive infinitesimal and intrinsically different from every other self." In making this distinction, Hopkins is not trying to separate the self into two parts. There is only one existing self, but if we are to do justice to it, we have to think of all that goes to make it up, what he calls the nature, which is of a determinate kind, and the "I," free and active, which does in fact create something out of what is our nature. This it is which makes human beings responsible beings who mean what they say, do what they do, and call their will their own. Some years ago there was a report in a usually accurate magazine of a child (or children) born with two heads. It or they lived for some months, and certainly long enough for evidence to be forthcoming of the clash of two wills, though the body below the heads was common property. This intrinsic positiveness, Hopkins contends, is displayed only in a rational free being. That is to say, he wanted to bring to light what is presupposed when we say that a human being is free. Two eggs, if precisely alike, would continue to develop in like conditions in an identical way. Where there is a human being, there could be no such certainty. This shows that there is another factor at work which can choose alternatives within the circumscribed field of the nature it has. Hopkins himself uses this word "field" in which the free self can play. He gives it the name "pitch" to indicate the core of its being, where its freedom is exercised.*

---

* Lest the reader grow impatient at the idea of this self which is "a zero in the score of its existence" and only positive as a "possible," let me point out to him that there is a noticeable likeness between what Hopkins wrote and the analysis of the self made by Heidegger and Sartre and Merleau-Ponty. He seems to have anticipated their insight in part. They distinguish human beings from real objects in that other objects are what they are, whereas a

Hopkins gives us a clue here to why persons, no matter what their gifts or education or success in life, put so much stress upon their own opinions, rights, and freedom. There are obvious difficulties in this account, an overemphasis, perhaps, on the positiveness of what cannot, as he says himself, exist by itself. There are also other sides of the self which he ignores. But, as I hope will become clearer at the end, what he says enables us to understand why it is that we are so in the dark about who we are and why the word "person" is so mixed up with masks. Again on Hopkins' premises, we can move forward to understand the special nature of human relations and how it is that men can keep themselves to themselves and at the same time surrender themselves to a cause or seek,

---

human being finds that he is a possible, that is, he has to make himself, and in his freedom there are various possibilities open to him. He is by his consciousness and freedom outside himself—a condition they describe as ek-stase. The pity is that man never can fulfil himself, and death ends the useless attempt. Now Hopkins, also, sees "the self as having the free power to make itself"—and so he distinguishes between the self and the nature which it has to adorn. One man starts with all the gifts of fortune, another is handicapped, but each has his field of play in which he exercises his freedom.

In both views, then, things are what they are and just that, but we are not what we are but what we do in our freedom. Many consequences may follow from this truth, if truth it be. In a sense we never are ourselves until united to others and to Another. We can fatally "lose our souls," and that will mean not being at home in our only habitation and so at a loss in ourselves and with others. Hell could signify the loss of identity, the split-self and friction within. Even the thought of the transmigration of souls may have behind it some such felt distinction and be due to a misinterpretation of the distinction between freedom of pitch and freedom of field.

like some mystics, to immerse themselves in the infinite. These are questions which have vexed thinkers for centuries, and they are part of a bundle of problems which are closely connected. What is this self which is always struggling for its own existence and at the same time prepared to sacrifice itself for others? In terms of love, this is the problem of self-interest and self-giving. Allied with this is the problem of what it means to love God and whether we can love God more than ourselves. The answer to these questions, I knew, should throw more light upon this mysterious self of ours.

IV

IN LOVING

WHEN I was a young priest, a distinguished Swedish theologian had challenged the traditional Catholic teaching on love in a work of three volumes called *Eros and Agape*. All the bees in my bonnet were stirred to activity by it and finally settled down into a book called *The Mind and Heart of Love*. Nygren claimed that a view of love alien to that of the Gospels had crept into Christian theology and had prevailed until Luther saw the light again. This alien view was a Greek intruder, and its name was Eros. Eros is always, on final analysis, a self-regarding form of love. In our vulgar loves we are on the make and out for pleasure, but even in its highest altitudes this kind of love is a form of having or possessing. Hence, to the Greek, perfect life will consist in happiness, the *beata vita* of Dante, the vision and enjoyment of God for all eternity. The view is based on the Aristotelian theory of life and living growth. Everything in a living organism is directed to the perfect functioning of the organism; this is what he calls its well-being or its "good." It follows that it is metaphysically impossible for the desire of an organism to reach beyond itself or against itself. To live, therefore, is to find what is "good" for the self. In conformity with this, Aristotle makes his divine being live in the serene contemplation of its own perfection without any interest in other beings. Now the early Fathers of the Church were naturally interested in finding in the cultural world around them what consorted with Revelation and helped to its elucidation. The one, however, most responsible for the wrong turning was, according to Nygren, St. Augustine. He had been trained in Neoplatonic thought and admired it all his life, and he inadvertently brought the language of Eros into Christian theology. The end of life from now on became to see and enjoy God. His influence was so great that the medieval scholastics carried on with his language. Aquinas, for instance, gives a full account of how the mind, uplifted by grace, is able to see God as He is and contemplate the divine essence in complete happiness. This grave mistake was only rectified at the Reformation by Luther, who restored the notion of Agape. According to Nygren, Agape is a new love revealed by Christ, God's own loving. Agape has no limits and is independent entirely of the merits of the recipient of it. "Your heavenly Father maketh his sun to shine on the evil and the good." It is summed up by Nygren under four heads. It is spontaneous and uncaused. It is indifferent to human merits. God does not love the good on account of their goodness. It is creative, so that independently of whether a man is good or bad, well disposed or evil disposed, he acquires value by the fact that he has become the object of Agape. Lastly it opens the way to friendship with God, and that friendship is due to grace and nothing else.

This view could never commend itself to me because it omitted so much in the New Testament which ran counter to it. The point of many of the parables turns on the notion of reward. Nygren had to confess that already in St. John's Gospel there are traces of what he calls Eros. But apart from scriptural objections, it makes an ugly break betwen human loving and divine loving, as if they had nothing to do with one another. Such a view can be necessitated only by an extreme theory of Original Sin, so making a calamitous division between our human life and the life of religious faith. Catholic theology does not accept any extreme theory of the utter corruption of human nature by Original Sin. Even in its exaggerated form, the distinction made by Nygren between the two loves had, all the same, an important bearing on the problem of human love as I saw it.

A clue as to how to get certain varying views on love into shape was provided in a book called *Passion and Society* by Denis de Rougemont. His thesis was a surprising one. What he called romantic love, so far from being a Christian growth, was the offspring of a once dangerous rival of Christianity called Gnosticism. We have been accustomed to thinking of romantic love as spiritual and chivalrous, knights wearing the gages of fair ladies, stories of courtesy and of Arthur and the Round Table. In fact courtly love broke up true marriage, and the love given to the fair maiden was not Agape, but Eros.

Christianity had made a sacrament of marriage. In it two were made holy in one flesh and one spirit. But there was another view of life which had penetrated into the Mediterranean and pretended to spiritualize Christian teaching. Time and time again it was condemned by the Church as it broke out sporadically in the Mediterranean basin. Its teaching came to this: that there were two principles, one good and the other evil. The soul belonged to the heavenly world, but to its misfortune, it was now imprisoned in the body. The flesh was evil, and the soul must seek salvation by avoiding marriage and turning to the night of death to be released and so find its way back to the realm of the spiritual and the divine. It is a religion of the dark, of the moon goddess, of mystic deaths. De Rougemont saw in this romantic movement an anti-human and an anti-rational movement, which belonged to the oriental, ecstatic type of religion, the type which oscillates between high mystical states and orgies of sensuality. In *The Mind and Heart of Love* I called this the feminine element in every human self and likened it to the unicorn charging wildly about until brought into obedience to divine love. In contrast with this feminine element is the masculine, which glories in reason, stands for law and order and the compatibility of spirit and matter. It is the Apolline attitude compared to the Dionysiac.

I have called the view of de Rougemont a clue, and so it is; for in following up what he said I saw how the self is composed of two main loves which can be called masculine and feminine. No doubt women manifest more frequently the tendencies which I have grouped under the word feminine but, as all will allow, women are quite as capable at times as men of displaying masculine tendencies. The masculine is masterful, possessive, and proud of exercising reason and self-control. The Aristotelian formula "to act according to right reason" was made for men; so too the advice to avoid excess, to show proportion and form in conduct and body. The feminine is not interested in these formulas. Its habit of soul is well expressed by March Phillipps in his *Form and Colour*. "The emotional mood, the mood of passive receptivity, in which insight is an integral part of feeling, is not only different from the rational and intellectual mood, but is itself dispelled by rational and intellectual definitions." To neglect either is to court disaster. If the self becomes self-centered, pride and egotism develop proportionately, and this inflation is usually followed by collapse. If on the other hand the self abandons itself to ecstatic love, it moves like a moth to the candle or, more passively, like the musk rose, it gives forth a stronger scent in the dark to entice a nightly robber visitant. Its joy is to be a victim, to belong to and become another.

These two loves are as constitutive of our being as our own two eyes and ears and legs are. They go into the makeup of other living species besides that of man. Half animal that we are, we can see how they work in those species, and what is thought brutal, bestial, and perverse in us, is natural to them. We borrow images from them to express these loves with their human expression, the bull and the ram and the cock and herds of cows and flocks of sheep. Mythology turns them into stories such as that of the Minotaur; and in the mad excesses of religion, we come across the Molochs and the Juggernauts, the Bacchants and the temple prostitutes. Santayana has described the two in a striking passage: "Apollo is the God of measure, perfection, of humanism. He is more civilized but more superficial, more highly conditioned . . . Yet the (Dionysiac) frenzy represents the primitive world-soul, not at home in the world, not settled in itself, and merging again with the elements, half in helplessness and half in transcendence and mystic triumph." Some may see in this the distinction Freud makes between the libido, which is an expression of the struggle for existence, and the death instinct. A full and proper human life consists in the balance between the need in a man to affirm his existence as an individual and the need to belong and to be accepted. Each need has its excellence which unfortunately can easily pass into a vice. The masculine in us asserts that we are persons and cannot be treated as means; that we have rights and claims, and no matter who or what we are, our privacy must be respected and our selfhood taken into account. The idea here is of a free individual playing a worthy part in life and, without obstruction, putting into practice his moral and religious ideals. But lest we extol the idea too much of a company of high-minded men walking down the street, fully aware of their own dignity, like Aristotle's "magnanimous man," and hardly bothering to say how do you do to the passerby, we have to be reminded that we belong to one another and that it is better to give than to receive. Here is mother love and family love and devotion to a cause and the humble giving and the practice of self-sacrifice, which has been the noblest characteristic of a man through history. This second love can be the wildest and most disruptive; it can also, when tamed like the unicorn, bring us nearer than the masculine love to the Agape of God.

In this life the peace between the two is an uneasy one; it is unmistakable evidence, like faith, of a higher life to come, when love will be all in all. We read of and thank God for perfect marriages and great friendships, like that of David and Jonathan. So much, however, has to be taken on trust, and not always is faith kept. Love itself can go astray as with Paolo and Francesca. Moreover, the saying, incomplete as it is, that each man is an island, has a true sense. Our inmost self is ours and no other human person's. No one can so penetrate into another's soul as to be utterly at one with him in all his thoughts, desires, pains, and joys as well as failings. We have no intuition of others, no more than we have the power to impart to others the whole of our experience, precisely as it is ours and no one else's. So it is that when we do what love calls upon us to do, that is, to give ourselves unconditionally, it is a leap in the dark, and willy-nilly there are understood reservations. We may have to put religion or country or plain duty at times above the demands of love. "I could not love thee, dear, so much, loved I not honour more." This shadow over all human loves points, as I have said, to a higher form of union, when all possible misunderstanding will have ended. God, as the Gospels teach, can love with a completely unselfish Agape because He has nothing to gain. (What He perhaps can gain is His own love in us washed with our tears and mottled with our unequal and wandering affection.) He has been upstairs and downstairs in the soul and knows every nook and dusty corner. Hence He is the only one who is in every moment of our lives co-conscious with us. The self, on its part, has no need of any reservations. All that we have and are belongs. There is no backward glance at what we are doing. Life is transposed into a higher key, and the self is in union with the divine love.

In *The Mind and Heart of Love* I attributed the love of self to the essential side of a living human being, and the self-sacrificing side to the existential. It seemed to make sense. All living organisms, to which amongst others the human being belongs, from the moment of their conception struggle for survival or life. The embryo grows and takes what is good for it and rejects what interferes with it or would harm it. Generalizing from this, we can say that living beings seek necessarily their own good. It is their nature or essence to do this. To say this is to do little more than repeat what we have been saying about the masculine love. Eros, in other words, is bound up with the realization of the animal's powers and nature; it is ultimately self-seeking.

Everything seems to be provided in this description, except one thing, and that is the most important of all. There are people who can hold their hearers spellbound while they tell of the feats they have done or the medical cures they have invented or the planes that will fly upside down and arrive back earlier than they started. There may seem to be nothing wrong with the paper drafts of such inventions. One questiton remains: did these feats really happen, these cures occur, these inventions work? Existence, then, has little or nothing to do with the makeup of the things described; it bears on whether the idea or scheme or cure is real or not. Now I exist and there are millions in the city around me who exist, and still more millions in the world, some of them passing out of existence at the very moment you read this sentence. My existence, therefore, is not mine in the sense that my essence is. It does not belong to me in the same way; indeed, we are near to being nothing and all that we do is under the shadow of death. Our death is imbedded in us, and we carry our winding sheet from the cradle. We are outside reality; we have to do something which will make us complete and, as the Existentialists would have it, especially Heidegger and Sartre, we can never be complete. We are *pour soi* and we can only become an *en soi* by becoming God. This is the *cri de coeur* of the Existentialists, the craving to belong, really to be something more than an aspiration to be blown out by death. I would prefer to use the language of contingence, and of how our existence marks our separateness from God and from all else as well as our dependence on God and our inborn desire to be in union with him. The symbol of this love is the altar of sacrifice. In the western hemisphere the note of individual happiness and progress is more prominent, be it in the practices of religion, capitalism in industry, democracy in politics, and the persistent struggle for rights and liberties. In the east, on the other hand, individual life does not appear to have the same importance and, in the superior philosophies of the great religions, the ideal to be sought by prayer and techniques is the transformation of the individual self into some superconscious reality. The Christian religion would lay claim to make the best of both loves. There are, for sure, dark nights and mystic states. These however are transient phases of purification and end in a superpersonal relation of the human being with a God of infinite love. The self is no longer self-regarding, but the love given back to it gives "life, and that more abundantly." As in loving companionship, each person's excellence and joy are enhanced, as human love might reach a climax in which life was more co-conscious than individual, so too in the final Christian Agape, a promise is fulfilled: we are to share the privilege given to the Son by the Father "that they should all be one, as we are one; that while thou art in me, I may be in them, and so they may be perfectly made one" (John XVII, 33).

The conclusions of *The Mind and Heart of Love* ended one period of excavation into the structure of the self, for my mind was turning towards certain problems connected with the New Testament and history. The connection, however, between this interest and my former ones was much closer than I realized at first. The New Testament problem concerned the so-called eschatological passages in it. These passages seemed at first sight to declare a rapid end of the world and, without a doubt, some of the early

Christians expected it in their own lifetime. What then was the relation of Christianity to history, and how far was the Christian expected to turn his back upon the world and reject *all* its values? I was then pushed farther back to ask about the destiny of the individual and of human society, its relation to the Kingdom of God, and what had all the human side of the self got to do with what St. Augustine called the Doctrine of the Two Cities? Were there lasting secular values independent of Christianity or theism, or might it not be that man could only find his real name and purpose in life in a Christian setting? With these ideas, some clearly and some obscurely in mind, I wrote *The Sense of History*. At a first glance the Christian religion seems to lay such stress in its Creed on the other world that a man might excusably think that there was nothing very important in this life to do beyond saving his soul, by loving God and by loving his neighbor. On the other hand there grew up a compendium of philosophy which argued that independently of revelation man could reach truth, enjoy natural goodness, act freely, and survive after death. No more was said than that in theory man could do all this. In fact, however, we are entitled to hold that man has never been without grace of some kind, that he has been from the beginning of time watched over by a loving Providence, and that the special Providence which guided the "chosen people of Israel" was to be of benefit in the end to all the world. If throughout history, it was legitimate to believe that all the ordinary efforts of human beings were being drawn up into a higher order of excellence, it was also sensible to suppose that the Kingdom of God itself was not being created in a vacuum, but operated in and through our human roundabout. The saint as much as the sinner had to put on his workman's clothes and get on with his job.

To take first the question of the Second Coming. My interests at the time when this problem first confronted me were more philosophical than theological, and I settled it satisfactorily in my own mind without being aware that some scriptural scholars had already arrived at not too dissimilar conclusions. In what is called its prophetical and its eschatological literature, the Hebrew mind does not work by dates and times as a modern historian would do. The passages in the Gospels and the references in the rest of the New Testament dealt with a divine event, an "act of God." This event is of such gigantic impact upon mankind that it can be interpreted in many ways and seen fulfilled in different moments. Primarily it is to be seen as God's loving power and judgment operating in the life of every individual and in the saving of human society. It, so to say, ricochets in time. The Second Coming, the last day, the final judgment, sums up the manner of this encounter between God and His people. God is not to be seen in history, but He is operative all the while in that He faces us with decisions that mean to us everlasting life or death. For this reason the Gospels tell us that we are always to be on the lookout for His coming, with loins girt and lamps in our hands, ever watchful like the wise virgins, lest we be surprised as by a thief in the night. The encounter is likely to be unexpected; Jerusalem did not know the time of its visitation. In every generation the individual will have his opportunities and moments of crisis; and these moments will be choices involving grace, conversion, special calls, forgiveness, death, and final judgment. These are all parts of the same divine event or redemptive wooing of mankind by Christ, as the light of the sun produces different effects in the atmosphere and through the clouds. In history this coming is to have one outstandingly recognizable trait. Christ, in a true sense, is the fulfilment of history. He is called the "pleroma," and all that has been, or will be, is recapitulated in Him. The possibility that history might be meaningless, or that it might come to a bad end, is over. The Redemption signifies that the way is open to every individual to come to a perfect ending. Years later Dr. Robinson, now Bishop of Woolwich, expressed this neatly in the following words: "The Christian knows that the move that decides the games has already been played. Since the Resurrection of Jesus Christ, there can in fact be no other outcome to the contest. It is the period of the end-game. The enemy may go on redisposing his pieces as he wills. But the issue is now foreclosed, however delayed the finish may be. The end can bring nothing new; the final checkmate will simply translate into universal acknowledgement what is already a *fait accompli* in the finished work of Christ." This victory, however, has a special mark, which, as I have said, is recognizable. The mark is this, that this society of the new Christian people must follow the pattern of the Christ life. His victory is comprised in two scenes, the Passion and Death and the Resurrection, and these two parts of the Redemption are inseparable. It follows that the life of the individual and of the sacred community is a death in life and a life in death. The gist of this is put in one of the ancient songs of the Church, now to be found in the Sequence of the Easter Mass: "Death and life have met in battle wondrous to see. Lo, the Lord of Life is slain, but is alive and victor." The symbol of the Christian religion is the Cross, and paradoxically it is a joyous symbol. Each person has to come to the knowledge of this truth by tasting of bitter herbs and in the mark of suffering. An onlooker can suddenly realize it, as obviously Gerard Hopkins did when he read of the wreck of the *Deutschland* and the death of five Franciscan nuns drowned in the storm. Contained in this story, he wrote, is a truth that "few know" for here even "the faithful waver and the faithless fable and miss." They do not know that the Coming of Christ is now "lightning and love, a winter and warm," for Thou hast "Thy dark descending and most art merciful then."

Does it follow from this doctrine of suffering that the Christian must look upon this world as a wasteland and, so far as he can, keep his distance from it? Bonhoeffer and others take the opposite line, saying that what is called the supernatural must be absorbed into the secular. The tradition of the saints, of preachers and spiritual books through the centuries should give the lie to this; holy men, even senators, in Roman times rushing off to the Egyptian desert; hermits in cells; Celestine relinquishing the Papacy to go back to his mountain retreat; mystics who write about "clouds of unknowing," and finally the very prayers of the Church that we should disregard earthly and love heavenly things. Do not all these point to the need for the Christian to absent himself a while from human felicity? Certainly it would be a mistake to minimize the necessity of self-abnegation in the Christian religion. But then it should be remembered that in all great religions the call for self-denial is to be found—in some, indeed, in a far more unqualified way than in Christianity. To judge from past experience, man can get to no heights, physical, artistic, or moral, without it. In such a well-known philosophy of life as the Neoplatonic, there are, as in the east, techniques for changing the self into the likeness of what is One and Perfect. It could be argued that the spirit of asceticism in the first centuries of Christianity was partly due to this Neoplatonic influence. I do not think, however, that any such influence worked upon the Celtic Church in its love for fasts and penances in Ireland and Lindisfarne! There are, besides, all the "hard sayings" in the New Testament to be taken into account. No, a solution, if there be one, must be sought in the very center of the Christian faith.

To get the proportion right we must go back to essentials. Human living itself is such an obstacle race that philosophers like Hegel and Marx have declared its very law is a dialectic. No sooner do we say or do something than its contrary is aroused and, by overcoming this, we arrive at a new unstable synthesis, which will straightway give rise to its opposite. St. Paul calls the Christian life a warfare and bids us always be in arms against the spirit of this world and the enemy within. It is quite possible, therefore, to take one's full part in human occupations and admire them and say of them as God said of His creation, "that it was good," and at the same time live a life of self-denial. It looks, indeed, as if the two went together. Moreover, if the critic of Christianity, not satisfied with this answer, points his finger at the extreme forms of self-denial practiced, we can always retort that human lovers have always been mad and that true love is synonymous with self-sacrifice. If a lover wishes to pour a vase of spikenard and precious ointments over the feet of the beloved, who is to say him or her nay, especially if it be God who is the object of the love? But on more common-or-garden grounds the Christian can claim that he ought to be as fond of this world, if not fonder, than his unbelieving friend. He can quote the beginning passage of the *Book of Genesis,* and he has accepted the astounding article of the Creed that God became man. If God did become man, then human nature and all that is connected with it take on a value, even if it had not had one before. The Eucharistic prayer attaches an old and a new excellence to human nature: "O God, who didst marvelously fashion the dignity of human nature and still more marvelously refashion it." The natural ties of family appear in the Ten Commandments, and they receive a new blessing in Mary's Motherhood of God and in the love revealed in the Gospels which existed between Christ and his apostles and disciples. Such tender affections are not consonant with a puritanical outlook. Again, in the parables and in the Sermon on the Mount, such a love of nature is evinced that it is not surprising to find St. Francis speaking to living creatures as if they were his brothers and sisters. Many saints have had their pets and artists have called upon all the beauties of nature to celebrate the great mysteries of the Christian religion. It would seem, therefore, far more in accord with the Christian spirit to regard nature and the use of it as sacramental, as if throughout nature there could be found symbols which take fire and light up the mystery of God and His relationship with us. Nature is not outside the providential intentions of God, for through the Redemption, St. Paul says, all things are reorientated to a new order and headship in Christ.

The impulse to fly this world and purify soul and body is, nevertheless, too deeply implanted in the human heart to be dismissed as a pathological symptom or malaise. It keeps recurring and exists even among the wise. The so-called escapism of Thomas à Kempis is to be found in Marcus Aurelius and other wise pagans. The radical incompleteness of human life and its transiency give us check. There is so much preparation in youth, so many ideas and hopes open up before us as we come to manhood; and then hardly have we had time to look around and to try our strength when it is time to depart. Some lines written a few days before he was killed in the Dardanelles and found amongst his remains tell us of this feeling.

> Was it so hard Achilles, so very hard to die?
> Thou knowest and I know not—so much the
> happier I.
> I will go back this morning from Imbros o'er the sea;
> Stand in the trench, Achilles, flame-capped and shout
> for me.
>
> *Patrick Shaw Stewart*

Every literature has this same kind of refrain or weeps over the loss of some Lycidas. So fast do the joys of this world pass that they seem to be intimations of something more real and abiding than real themselves. I know that to talk the language of "real" and "more real" is dangerous and out of fashion; they do, nevertheless, stand for what generations have felt, the old and the young, the wise as well as the foolish. All have been persuaded of some relationship between the passing things of time and a place "yonder" of unchangeable perfection.

Those who do turn to the contemplation of what is "yonder" tell us that we have to discipline and purify our desires in the same kind of way in which we come to learn the difference between the trombones of a Sousa march and the organ notes of a Bach. Our human condition is not static; we can improve or deteriorate; and wise, saintly persons have handed down to us means and techniques for attaining holiness. Some of these techniques can produce startling results; but I am not thinking of those who acquire extraordinary powers over their bodies, nor again of the mystics who suffer ecstasies and may be raised above the ground. The quintessential improvement lies in the emancipation of the will and in the mastery of our passions, so that we can love without compromises or self-consciousness and hold steadfastly to the truth; and this is a lifetime's hard work.

Here then is one form of self-denial, which most would accept as necessary. But we have to go further than this. Take this dialectic already mentioned, which comes from our nature being in discord with itself; take saws and proverbs and aphorisms as evidence: "All power corrupts . . ."; "the fascination of trifles obscures the good"; the rich man and the eye of a needle. This discord shows itself in the conflict between concupiscence and gentle love, animal and spiritual tastes, and the selfish and unselfish impulses. In the more ancient schools of education, the use of the rod may have been exaggerated, but it testified to the unruly element in the young.

So far what I have been saying about discipline and spiritual warfare would hold for all mankind and is not specifically Christian. It needs stating, therefore, that Christians are sworn in by their very baptism to a special form of self-sacrifice. In the Gospels they are told they should be perfect even as their heavenly Father is perfect. That in itself is new and sublime. But they are also bidden to put on Christ, and this does not mean an instruction just to behave like Christ. The union which Christ asks for and has promised to create is a union such that the individual can call himself Christ. He takes on in a mysterious way a new form of life with the result that, like St. Paul, he can say: "I live, no, no longer I, for Christ lives in me." That this is to be taken seriously is shown by the images which St. Paul uses to illustrate his teaching. We are regenerated or born again; we are heirs, co-heirs with Christ, sons of God, members of Christ, members of a body whose head is Christ, and so on. In the fourth Gospel the striking image of the vine and its branches is used: "I am the vine and you are the branches." The truth contained in this teaching is at the end beyond full comprehension, for it entails that we are raised to the level of the divine life itself, while at the same time we keep our own personality.

Christian living consists in "suffering" and cooperation in this change-over. The transformation is bound to be painful, for as I have written in another place: "Just as after the introduction of a foreign body into an organism, there is a period of pain and friction before absorption, so too the supernatural life has slowly to dominate and fuse with the natural, and nature is at first recalcitrant. In fact, the process of fusion is hardly ever accomplished before death, and the ecstasy of the saint bears witness as much to the unsubdued condition of the body and lower faculties as to his union with God." This transformation can be compared also to the consuming of wood or coal in a fire, and this image gives one an idea of the true meaning of self-denial and self-sacrifice; for it is an ordeal to step onto a pyre, even though it be an affair of love and at the end means union with God himself.

There is still a coda I must add to this discussion on self-denial. The passages about the coming of Christ are concerned, as already mentioned, with the fate of the individual and with the new Christian society. They brought out the teaching of the New Testament about the special honor and glory of each individual soul. Each person is a miniature cosmos, and he is given opportunities of committing himself and of making decisive choices. C.S. Lewis has said of man that "each one finds in his own life every moment of time is completely filled. He is bombarded every second by sensations, emotions, thoughts which he cannot attend to for their multitude, and nine-tenths of which he must simply ignore. A single second of lived time contains more than can be recorded. And every second of past time has been like that for every man that ever lived." This does not mean a long and unimportant story of missed opportunities; it is rather a reminder of the enormous importance of each moment in the life of a person. Hegel saw historical occasions as "moments" in the sweeping movement of Universal Spirit, and one wave is subsumed into another wave, helps its impetus but disappears itself. It is in this way that we are inclined to think of individuals when reading history or a novel. The vast hordes of the east come across the horizon and vanish again like Parthians shooting backwards as they ride away beyond capture or recognition. In nearer times the crowds besieging the Bastille or gathering in front of the Palazzo Venetia have no face, and even those mentioned by the historians are so colored and stylized that they remain as mysterious as the Mona Lisa.

We know, however, from our own experience, that we each have a private view, and in this the world orbits round us. Nobody else can see the world for us, let our experience be as trivial and transient as you will; and when we die, we are stone dead. The Christian view does not fit in with this at all. We think of ourselves and of others as moving towards some almost predetermined ripeness, as we watch an ugly duckling turn into a swan. Ripeness is all; we develop, play our part, and then in our obituary notice, we are judged on what we have been in the main. The Christian emphasis, on the contrary, is on the now, for now is the acceptable time, now is the crisis and all depends on our response. Hence it is that inscriptions on tombstones are often more worthy than accurate. They imply that because the cobbler or the squire has on the whole been a decent man and done a decent job, he is now sharing in the joys of heaven. This comfortable doctrine may well be an understatement; certainly it leaves out of account the story of the Good Thief and it ignores the truth that one act of love can abolish a thousand sins. Let us grant that we do develop from infancy to manhood, and during the period of formation, we are not sufficiently ourselves to be fully accountable for our actions. This is all preliminary to a time when we have done sucking and can no longer make excuses. Once we are fully in possession of our will and mind, once we can reflect and act freely, we sign our own checks and can sign away our fortune and our lives. We go on changing, but it is a process of consolidation more than becoming something new. We have to be judged now, not in the light of some performance to come, as if we were still sparring before going into the ring. At each moment we are complete; we risk our good name, and we show ourselves for what we are. It is on these grounds that theologians say that we can choose to make an act of love or to commit a grievous act and fix our destiny forever.

A distinction made by Aristotle elucidates what I have just written. There are processes, he says, which have no significance or value except in the result. These are to be seen all round us in the physical world and in the laboratories of scientists or industrial factories. A good dish may look an awful mess in the making, but in the end it is the chef's glory and the delight of those who eat it. In contradistinction to such processes, Aristotle calls a series of thoughts or acts of the will perfect or complete. The proper comparison here would be not to a dish but to a necklace of pearls or diamonds, each precious stone being valuable in itself. A grown-up person, therefore, lives by encountering reality, meeting it head on, and committing himself. This is man's prerogative, and it creates all the problems of community life, of the relation of the individual to society and the State. The autocratic State does not give an individual his proper rights, while on the other hand a democracy which veers towards anarchy gives the individual so much liberty that the community suffers. At its best the State conserves order and looks to the general welfare. It can do no more.

Some Christians believe in the union of Church and State; Bonhoeffer holds that the idea of the supernatural is outmoded and that we must look for God in the secular world around us. The attitude of the Existentialists in this matter seems to be ambiguous. To Kierkegaard religion is a matter of taking steps in the dark, walking out on wild waters like St. Peter in order to be at the side of Christ. This is neither secularist nor necessarily supernatural. What, however, may have served to weigh the scales against the supernatural is the agnosticism of Martin Heidegger and his preoccupation with death. We live, according to Heidegger, in the twilight of the gods, watching death creep up upon us. Death is like the ghost at the feast, and this sense of imminent death gives another sense to the Gospel images of the knock at the door and the thief in the night. As touching our mortality and human contingence, this "concern" is natural and it may warm the soul to rely upon God, as in the Psalms. It reappears in the Christian prayers as a warning not to build our house on sand or sit feasting with Baltassar or Dives, but "so to pass through temporal things that we do not forget heavenly things." It is only for those, therefore, who accept the "Being-towards-Death" view of human life that religion must bow to the decrees of this our mortality.

If Bonhoeffer errs on the side of secularism, Karl Barth is uncompromisingly against any commerce between the Word of God and the world's wisdom. He will admit no traffic between the divine and the human. Like his divine Master, he would drive all buyers and sellers out of the temple. God's revelation is a *mysterium tremendum* beyond human comprehension. All speech about it is a solecism, and faith is a pure gift bringing the promise of everlasting life; it bypasses human concepts and human moral ideals. The life of the Christian must consist in living by faith in another kingdom and finding true life there and not in this world. Barth himself tells us that the best that can be seen in the world is a reflection like the light on a pool or mountainside. All culture is "an exclusive earthly reflection of the Creation which itself remains . . . lost and hidden from us." There is "no continuity between the analogies and the divine reality; by reason of our divided self, but also for this further reason, that our self is not in accord with righteousness."

Those who sing this manner of song, as if they were living by the waters of Babylon, are worthy of the highest respect; they do keep before our minds the great contrasting themes of this "world" and the kingdom of God, nature and grace, time and eternity. But in the last century a new rich vein of thought has been opened up with the discovery of a new significance in change. Change is transformed by the discovery of evolution. It is not so much just turning one sod over another or changing streets and habitations; evolution and dialectic allow apparent opposites to meet, and from clash to emerge in new forms. No longer have we to think of the world of nature and living things as static; and if the world is on the move in a never ceasing ascent, why, as Teilhard de Chardin pertinently asked, should it not play its part in man's final dénouement?

One recalled Friedrich von Hügel's favorite theme of tension, of how we need the spur of risk and adventure to prevent us from falling asleep. Tension depends upon a motive and resistances. In medicine now this principle is applied in all sorts of ways; but in fact, once perceived, this principle or truth is seen to be universal. As a falcon cannot ride the air without resistance—its "hurl and gliding rebuffed the big wind"—nor a plane, so neither the senses in man nor the appetites, nor the teeth and digestive system can thrive without this friction. Such a law of nature is likely then to be operative in the spiritual life, and nature should play the part which fire does in making a candle burn and flame.

This form of cooperation through tension which the world can provide is not however sufficient of itself to settle this momentous question of the relation of the kingdom of God and the kingdom of man. Barth has done a needed work in freeing the faith from much of the comments and interpretation put upon it by liberal thinkers. It would, nevertheless, be a strange view of God to make

Him set aside as worthless His own creation and His own gift of knowledge to man. A theist ought not to tolerate such an idea, nor is there any good reason why it should be accepted. He may see man's own evil effects as a wasteland and admit the possibility that individual human beings may ruin themselves and end in spiritual bankruptcy. The evil that men do does live after them and spreads. This no doubt is the "world" which St. John has in mind when he says that it has no part with Christ. In his first letter he writes that "its gratifications pass away"; it offers "only gratifications of corrupt nature, gratifications of the eye, the empty pomp of living." It has been the duty of Christian preachers to warn their flocks of the many illusory pleasures of this world and of the fascination of evil, drawing men like a Circe to feast and become like swine. Moralists have had to do this from the beginning of human time, and the ideal put before the Christian is so high and pure that he must make special preparation and realize that in comparison with the love of God in Christ all else is as dross. At the same time the Christian faith cannot help bubbling over into the arts and sciences. There are moments, especially when a nation becomes grossly self-indulgent, when men like Savanarola pronounce the judgments of God on the evil doings of artists as well as of Borgia popes and drive a Botticelli to cast his paintings into the bonfire. Anything can happen in the strange story of man, but in fact all human actions in their right proportions can serve the great eucharistic mystery and enable human beings to give of their substance to the re-creation of human life. As I wrote in *The Sense of History*: "All human action prepares the way for the coming of Christ's kingdom. . . . Those who are in grace have an interior quality which gives a further dimension to their humanity . . . and it makes their work anticipatory of what is to come. Man's life on earth now is meant to fertilize the good seed of supernatural life. Time is the flower and eternity is the fruit."

As so often has happened to me, the thoughts I thought I discovered by myself and imagined to be original turned out to have been public property for a long while, or at least already to have been chalked out. In this case the view expressed above appears, though in a different context, in Newman's *Idea of a University*. There he insisted upon the intrinsic value of a high, humane education. "The Creator of the World is none other than the Father of our Lord Jesus Christ; here are not two worlds, one of matter and one of spirit; one of the Law and one of the Gospel. . . . We must not give up the visible world as if it came from the evil one. It is our duty to change it into the kingdom of heaven." He preached on "God's temporal blessings" in his *Sermons of the Day* and told his congregation that "all the beauty of nature, the kind influence of the seasons, the gifts of sun and moon and the fruits of the earth, the advantages of civilized life, and the presence of friends and intimates; all these good things are but one extended and wonderful type of God's benefits in the Gospel. Those who aim at perfection will not reject the gift, but add a corrective. They will add the bitter herbs to the fatted calf and the music and the dancing; they will not refuse the flowers of earth, but they will toil in plucking out the weeds."

St. Paul is many-sided, but he too seems to have taken a cosmic view of the change wrought by Christ's coming. "Created nature," he told his Roman friends, "has been condemned to frustration, not for some deliberate fault of its own, but for the sake of him who so condemns it, with a hope to look forward to, namely, that nature in its turn will be set free from the tyranny of corruption to share in the glorious freedom of God's sons." This mysterious reference to the setting free of nature was not fully appreciated by the early Christians in their expectation of a rapid, if not almost immediate, end of the world. They were so conscious of the new life given to them in baptism and the eucharist that the old seemed dead and gone, and they took no thought of the future. Now was the acceptable time; next day might be the "day of the Lord." Time went on, and gradually the rich complexity of the Second Coming came to be understood better. But what with their fugitive life in the catacombs and their long endurance of mad or persecuting emperors, they were not greatly interested in the riches of the world, its history and what they might signify to them. They worked in the heat of the sun wondering whether they would see a new dawn. But as the centuries passed, they could stop to look at the work they had done and at the world around them. And what a work that was! A new cosmos larger than that of the Roman Empire, possessing the order of the Empire, with the tribes which had destroyed it now turned into spiritual legions. The learning of the old academies had passed into the monasteries and the cathedral schools, and from them emerged the ideal of university life. Christianity and human learning had joined hands.

A better understanding of the peculiarities of the Hebrew way of looking at history and at life has dissipated some of the objections which have been raised against this too worldly view of Christianity. The Hellenic world, as P. Daniélou has pointed out, made a sharp distinction between "divine things" which are everlastingly the same, without beginning or end, and lesser realities which are corruptible and must therefore end even as they began. Possessed of such a frame of mind, the learned, when confronted with a religion which ignored these necessities and took time seriously and brought the everlasting down to earth, were shocked. This new Christian religion, sprung out of Jewry, taught that history under the direction of Yahweh moves forward to a finale, and a theme is developed in time which is nevertheless incorruptible. Again the apocalyptic literature struck those trained in Greek thought as monstrously odd, for here was a theme which kept repeating itself with multiple variations and making its presence felt in moments of time. To Oscar Cullman the credit must be given of clarifying definitively the differences between Greek and Hebrew attitudes of mind. The Greek, he tells us, had a cyclical view of history, whereas the Hebrew thought in terms of an ascending straight line. The Greek desires to get out of time: "I have escaped from the wheel of fate," as an Orphic tablet is inscribed. To the Jew, salvation is in history due to God's intervention in it. The Lord Kurios has control of human events, and by his death and resurrection, he has won a decisive and conclusive victory. So conclusive is this victory that in Cullman's eyes the period after the victory is quite different from that which preceded it. He calls it the "interim" period and says that its purpose is to allow the conquest of matter by the spirit. It is the last hour and is accompanied by signs, the while missionaries go forth to the ends of the world to announce the good news.

Surprisingly, Cullman does not draw the conclusion from his analysis of Jewish ideas that history and the world of nature have their part in this "interim." To him, "the figure of this world passes." It is at best a framework which is needed if Christians are to live their lives as citizens and in fellowship with one another. Such a judgment seems to minimize the work of the Kurios who, as he himself has asked us to believe, is the Lord of history. Why, if this be so, exclude secular history and nature? The eschatological elements in the Gospels and further explanation of them in St. Paul point to a richer conception of the "interim" period. Its purpose is not so much to give time for the "conquest of spirit over matter" as to allow the whole world to come under the dominion of Christ. Moreover, that same Christ who wore a Syrian smock and spoke with a Galilean accent is, in the Pauline belief, in his risen life the cosmic Christ who draws into his life and new body all worthwhile human experience. For this to happen, time is needed for man to get all that is possible out of himself and of nature. The difference in man's experience at the time of Christ, at the Renaissance, and now is so vast as to enable us to see how necessary time is for the incorporation of all things in Christ to take place. Only within living memory have primitive societies in far parts of the world come to be known; so recently again have they learned civilized ways and put on sovereignty. We live still in an unfinished universe, and there is still the possibility of a world-wide understanding and peace. Such hopes for the future must be entertained by a Christian philosopher, and later I will try to show more precisely the meaning of this doctrine of "incorporation."

As regards human values, Cullman treats them as tools which are finally to be left behind when the Lord of history comes to make his victory complete and everlasting.

This too is a disappointing comment on the work of a man who goes out in the morning to sow with tears and comes back in the evening rejoicing as he carries his sheaves with him. What Cullman calls "interim" might with greater truth be called sacramental, if that word be taken not too technically. Loss and gain, death and life are our lot, and we have to make the best of it, but there has always been a faint hope amongst men that what is lost might not be lost for ever and that somehow the fragrance of the experience might be preserved as incense. God, who is outside time in, as Boethius describes it, "the full and immediate and perfect possession of unending life," has no such finite experience. It is said too that a pure spirit would be so perfect all at once as never to need to progress by gain and loss. Such a being would be like Emily Dickinson's wind "that rose, though not a leaf in any forest stirred." Poor as our human condition is, subject to space and time, it has its own peculiar beauty, the "momentary happiness of mortal men." Such a state inevitably implies imperfection, and a critic might ask how can work and conduct, which even at their best always bear the smudge of time and imperfection upon them, be taken up into the life of Christ and become part of the City of God? The difficulty rests partly on the assumption that the City of God to which we hope to belong will come into existence at the end of time. But for all we know, the heavenly society is already being formed, or the end of the world has already come. The important point, therefore, is that our experiences should in fact be transfigured, not *when* they are transfigured. Everything which happens in time is equidistant from God, as the circumference is from the center. God, indeed, should be thought of rather as in the center of our souls than distant; he shares all the individual's secret thoughts and private acts. If then all that we are and do is always present to God, there is no reason why the cosmic Christ should not embody them, and present them to the Father of all good things. Abbot Butler of Downside put this neatly when he wrote that we do not go to our meeting with God without luggage. Many have felt that they expressed themselves in some great act or choice in their lives; others have found themselves in some emergency; others again must have relived certain moments, Archimedes and Galileo and Newton in their discoveries, the first poet who saw his beloved as a red, red rose.

Not all, of course, can be considered worth preserving or remembering; the skeletons in our cupboards will not rattle in the new life. Apart from what is really evil, there is much that is frivolous or routine or impersonal, much that is crude and tentative. History is strewn with the bones of poor or immature ideas and performances. Let us grant that at the last day there will be a vast rubbish heap and the last man to survive can put a match to it. But of the rest? To a supreme connoisseur like God, everything in our lives must look like a junk shop or one of those areas where broken down motor cars lie in profusion. But this will not do because we are told in the Gospels that it is the weak who will inherit the kingdom before the strong, and in the parable the weak and the halt are invited to the feast. So there is reason to think that everything which is free of evil can be graced and transfigured.

If we change our rather stiff image of heavenly bliss and suffer it to be human as well as celestial, there is nothing to prevent our smuggling in there what might startle at first sight some of the desert fathers. Our standards of what is great and small, serious and light, may not apply in the presence of God. Suppose then that we surrender all claims to model conduct and edifying virtues and lay the stress on that special finite quality of our experience which, while always imperfect, is dear to us as human beings. We can always admire absolute standards and try to reach them; but the mass of our experiences do not amount to very much if weighed against absolutes. What makes our neighbor so friendly and companionable may seem trifling; but these trifles are like the toys which children love and take to bed with them. "Take these imperfect toys, till in your heart they too attain the form of perfect things"; perfect things which have become so in the atmosphere of heaven. In this way the green fields of which we babble when we die are not far from the "green pastures" to which we hope to go.

Most of us have to confess that we have never done anything memorable in our lives; they are just a string of small events no more world-shattering than having a tooth out. Nevertheless, as H.G. Wells once wrote, everyone feels that he is a man of destiny: "what a man shall this be, for the hand of the Lord is with him." He feels that he is sure before he dies to be like the man in the fairy story who is changed into the prince and has his day of glory. One of the joys of the Christian Revelation is that it assures us that there is an element of truth in this belief. Every individual is a prince or king in disguise, Davids tending their flocks who shortly will smite a Goliath and be anointed king of Israel. We only see with our mortal eyes the graveyards which do not give up their secrets, but there is a basis for the belief that the good is not interred in the grave, and that not one of the innumerable small acts done in grace vanishes into nothingness, certainly not the successes and failures, partings and reunions, laughter and tears of our common humanity. The Greeks have left us a record of much that is moving and tender in their epitaphs and verses to be found in the Greek Anthology. If art can make an everlasting sonnet or scene out of transient incidents or gestures, why should not the grace of God transfigure what is homely and bittersweet? Hence we may expect that the human *commedia* with its tangled mass of bittersweet experiences will, with the exception of what is rotted with evil, receive a divine benediction.

The description "bittersweet" is used with deliberation because it expresses a distinct characteristic of human life; that is, the combination of joy and sorrow at its fleetingest. It is epitomized in the famous lines of Nashe written in time of plague:

> Beauty is but a flower
> Which wrinkles will devour:
> Brightness falls from the air;
> Queens have died young and fair;
> Dust hath closed Helen's eye;
> I am sick, I must die—
> Lord, have mercy on us!

This strange mixture of intense pleasure mixed with melancholy has something in common with the "tension" already mentioned and the pain and joy found in encountering resistances. "There is no poppy in Castile so lovely as his open wound." We think of the perfect man on the balcony of Pilate's palace: *Ecce Homo,* the crowns of thorns and the crowns of glory. What is called "bittersweet" is the subjective side of the struggle for existence and life; it is also the mark of Christ's coming, which christens "the wild worst best." Above all is this characteristic demonstrated in self-sacrifice, where the two loves are operative and the self is at its best in giving its all.

As a summary of all my thought on this mysterious self that man possesses, I cannot do better than quote from *The Meaning and Matter of History*. "The eschatological point of view threw a light on the chief actor in history, the individual himself. Each individual is a miniature cosmos, and the whole earth and all time draw near to force the decisive yes or no from him. Time in a sense stands still because it has been fulfilled in Christ, and every individual and every generation lives at the end of the world meeting his destiny. This, it has been claimed, is a unique contribution of Christianity to the philosophy of history, but while it explains the individuals who compose history, it leaves out of account the growth which in time man and mankind have achieved in community, in nation, and as a whole. The question, therefore, can be asked whether all the human achievements and the struggle and development are just a waste product, or have they any everlasting significance? Do they enter into any scheme whose nature can be seen or surmised? In another form the question comes to this: has the development of the city of man any abiding relation with the city of God? That there is a city of God, which also is coming into being, is guaranteed by the New Testament and by Christian tradition. It must be accepted as a truth just as much as the eschatological fact. At first the difficulties in the way of knowing anything about the ultimate character of the city of God and about the relation of human experience to it seemed overwhelming." A possible answer has been given in the account just given of God's love for man in becoming man and reconciling man with himself. This victory has special characteristics; it manifests itself in every individual, providing opportunities and graces for decisive choices. The individual so chosen looms larger than life, even though his natural life be that of a pygmy. It manifests itself secondly in society in the building up of the city of God. The end of the world is in one sense already here, for the world dies for each individual when he dies, and each generation also passes away. More and more, however, do men make something of this world to their own enormous advantage in knowledge and human communication, so that the final end will not come until all that is rich in human experience has been incorporated into the life of the cosmic Christ. How can that be? So far as human truth and human goodness are concerned, there is no great difficulty. But for the mass of human experience as suffered and enjoyed by the underdogs of history? The answer to their predicament, it has been suggested, lies in the very imperfection of human temporal experience, for it is this bittersweet experience, which the Son of Man above all endured, and it is this which will be transfigured and give continuity to what happens now and what will be fastened to the tenderest truth in eternity.

V

MAKING UP WITH THE WORLD

In the first pages of this Credo, I remarked that each of us has a bent or master passion from the beginning and that it pulls us back from straying too far and blows its horn when we get on to the scent. Some few know what they want from the beginning; most of us only realize what we have been searching for when the game is almost over. I am speaking here not of the general outline of a philosophy to be lived but of the way we shape truths and have insights into them in accordance with our loves. The subject matter of a philosophy is distinct from that of the sciences in that it deals with what is always with us and will never change. Science leaps from hypothesis to hypothesis, whereas philosophy looks at the same subject, be it time or space or mind or love, human beings and ourselves and God, finding in the contemplation of them ever new aspects and ever new relations. Aristotle was at no disadvantage compared with us when he pondered over mind, and Sappho probably knew more about love than some of her modern commentators. It is in the systematizing, however, that the philosopher is most likely to go wrong. If the system be sound, it will surely happen that it will get thicker and thicker with meaning as the years go on. He will be introducing more and more livestock into his Ark. Owing to one's particular passion, it is natural that certain problems should take precedence over others. More and more the notion and value of the person has come into view, and there remains much more to be said about the relation of the person to God and whether for one's own proper self-realization a "sense" of God is necessary.

For many years now the problem of the self has lured me on. Could anything be more obvious? And yet like the unicorn of fable or the shy lizard on the rocks, it was most difficult to surprise and to see clearly. Moreover there was something disturbing in the fact that philosophic explorers had come back with such different tales to tell of the self. In the eyes of eastern sages, it had a tenuous hold on reality. Plato pictured it as a charioteer driving the inferior parts of itself; Aristotle called it the form of the body; Kant reduced it to being the transcendental subject of perception. Hegel thought of it as a passing moment in the concrete realization of the Spirit. And for a while the modern empiricists left it out of their philosophizing as an unnecessary extra. Old views which gave the learner the comfortable sense that he was somebody, even an immortal somebody, could be made to look antiquated in the light of modern psychoanalysis, the recent startling advances in surgery, and the researches into the working of the brain. Take, for instance, the original work of Freud or the experiments with new drugs. The descriptions of what happens after taking mescalin or LSD-25 have given the impression that one can have the highest spiritual experiences of the mystics and saints by consuming a tiny particle of black fungus. True it is that if we look more closely at these states of consciousness we find that they do no more than simulate the intense feelings of the mystic; they have no spiritual content and no beneficial result. Nevertheless they are so near to the truth that they give encouragement to scientists who forget the warning of Dr. Robert S. De Ropp that "the scientist who attempts to study the chemistry of thought and feeling resembles a burglar attempting to open a vault of one of the world's major banks with a toothpick." At the same time let it be admitted that there is much that is new which calls for explanation. Parts of the brain which hitherto were unattainable because they were too deep to be reached can now be electrically stimulated, and it has been found that they are the physical sources of rage, placidity, pleasures, pains, and sexual feelings. There is therefore a temptation among empirical scientists to essay an entirely physical explanation of all the conduct of the self, and of the self. They pass from the legitimate rubric of their profession, that only what can be observed and tested has meaning for them, to denying that there is anything else beyond what they can see and touch. Their findings cannot be ignored, but their inferences will not hold water; and this can be shown quite simply. A scientist of repute, and one-time atheist, J.B.S. Haldane, can be called in to give evidence of this. In an article written many years ago for the *Outline,* he began by saying how unwilling he would be to support any religious view of man which held him to be immortal. He ended, however, by writing that "in order to escape from the necessity of sawing away the branch on which I am sitting, so to speak, I am compelled to believe that mind is not wholly conditioned by matter." The effects of drugs, he went on, alcohol, and disease are such indeed as to prove that the limitations of his own finite and imperfect "mind" are "largely at least due to the body. Without that body, it may perish altogether, but it seems to me quite as probable that it will lose its limitations and be merged into an infinite mind or something analogous to a mind, which I have reason to suspect probably exists behind nature. How this might be accomplished, I have no idea."

We are not told whether this mind is moral, evil, or neutral. What he is sure of is that the mind in us must not be confused with the brain or anything physical; and the reason he gives is clear enough and decisive. He argues that if the mind and the brain were one and the same, then he would be "sawing away the branch on which I am sitting." In other words, if my statement is of the same order as a physical movement, then it loses its quality of saying anything which is true and undetermined by its material cause. M. Merleau-Ponty in his *Phenomenology of Perception* also rules out physical explanations of mental acts but on phenomenological grounds. About perception, for example, he writes that empirical psychologists make it up out of states of consciousness as a house is built with bricks. A mental chemistry is invoked which fuses these materials into a compact whole. But all they are doing is describing blind processes which could never be equivalent to knowledge, because in this mass of sensations and memories there is *nobody* who sees, nobody who can appreciate the falling into line of datum and recollection. . . . To perceive is not to experience a host of impressions accompanied by memories capable of clinching them; it is to see standing forth out of a cluster of data an imminent significance without which no appeal to memory would be possible. The scientist without realizing what he is doing transforms the self as subject, the I who is experiencing and making knowledge possible, into an object, a third reality, which is proved to be incapable of being an active knowing subject. The living body becomes an exterior without interior, and the self becomes an external spectator or a ghostlike subject without any status. So the self turns into a hybrid, an empirical self and a subjective principle of thought. The self which is the creation of the scientific thinkers devours itself by making itself a morsel to eat; and, of course, somehow or other the mouth and the digestive organs have become part of the morsel. I have already quoted Haldane on the suicidal nature of the materialist's conclusions. C.S. Lewis puts the same kind of objection in his own vigorous way. "Scientific cosmology won't do because it leaves no room for reason or independent mind. . . . If I swallow the scientific cosmology as a whole, then not only can I not fit in Christianity, but I cannot even fit in science. If minds are wholly dependent on brains and brains on biochemistry and biochemistry (in the long run) on the meaningless flux of the atoms, I cannot understand how the thoughts of those minds should have any more significance than the sound of the wind in the trees."

The recognition that mind cannot be reduced to body nor body to mind only serves to open up new problems. Philosophers can still shade off into a semi-materialism or pseudo-idealism. Within recent years interest in this subject has revived amongst certain analytical and linguistic philosophers. So for me to achieve some kind of stance before the world I tried to understand as *true*, I had to face up to their visions of the universe and work through them to mine. For some years their school of thought had, as I have said, resembled a post office which sees that letters are properly stamped and rightly addressed, but tells one nothing of the content of the letters, as they bear on individual, family, social, national, or international life. (Unlike Thomism, there did not seem to be any place for letters to go.) Their service, therefore, had not been of much direct use to those seeking for a philosophy which could be lived. Gilbert Ryle, for example, directed most of his fire against those who regarded mind as a kind of "ghost in the machine" (each of these two nouns is weighted). He has, I think, the Cartesian tradition in mind, a tradition which stands for two levels in the self and a central point of communication somewhere in the body. He is also critical of the bad habit we have of thinking of what unifies constituents as something extra outside the constituents. Thus we tend to think of a college or government, a state or nation as something existing in itself over and above the constituents. Ryle argues that if we remove many of the confusions in our thinking, we shall find that there is no need to postulate an interior world of thinking and desiring. All can and should be brought out into the open. "I try to show that when we describe people as exercising qualities of mind we are not referring to occult episodes of which their overt acts and utterances are effects; we are referring to these overt acts and utterances themselves." These remarks look harmless, but that is only because Ryle has so framed them that he might well be saying only the obvious. No one would disagree with him when he says that in "exercising qualitites of mind, we refer to the outward expression of them," if he means by "exercising" talking, speaking, or writing. The question is whether in saying "that was a good speech," "a good paper," "a fine effort," we never imply that much quiet thought must have gone into the making of the speech or that the speaker may have other versions of it which he may some day use. There seems to be no account taken of the hours spent by men and women in contemplative orders in silent meditation, nor of those troubled persons who have repressed thoughts for so long that they have to seek help from a psychiatrist to bring them back to utterance. Ryle must be fully aware that we always take for granted that a person in a prepared speech must have given thought beforehand to what he is saying, and even in ordinary conversation we make a distinction between what a person may be saying and what he is intending to say, but not in fact uttering; for we often ask "Is that what you mean?" or "Do you really mean what you are saying?"

Ryle could reply that the thinking and the expression are the same and that the distinction made between them is artificial. Many a young artist would vigorously deny this, but let us grant that he has a point here and that we do tend to exaggerate at times the two-sidedness of our considered actions. We are reminded as well that introspection is a giddy business even though it must be the ultimate guarantee that the experience is our own. We are warned by spiritual writers not to overdo introspection, and it is good to find Ryle on their side! Too much staring disturbs the interior landscape, and can lead, as with introverts, to illusions. But surely Ryle goes too far, for we have to examine our motives and try our best to "say what is in our minds." This ability, which is requisite for any honest intercourse with others and for our own search into philosophic truth, can go with a certain degree of ignorance of our own selves. Ryle, however, seems to be more intransigent, for he leaves it doubtful whether he believes in mind at all. He goes so far as to write of the "myth of consciousness," saying that it is "a piece of para-optics." But that is not Ryle at his best, and it may be that his stress on behaviorism is deliberate in order to get rid of "private" views and "private" worlds. There is no such thing as "a privileged position"; we are all in the same world watching a piece of behavior, and the feelings of Floyd Patterson being knocked out in less than a minute are as open to all the spectators, ringside and television, as to Patterson himself. In support of his contentions, he reminds us that we are creatures of habit, and that we do not usually think about dressing in the morning or washing or how to eat; this habitual way of behaving is on all fours with physical habits; that is to say, that our habit of blowing our nose and being kind to others is the same. Again we have been under a delusion for centuries about the process of thinking. Our assumption that it consisted in forming ideas and then passing judgment is wrong; thinking is in fact a process like swimming or driving a car; the chief difference is simply that in thinking we are learning how to use words correctly. (There is no room in Ryle's philosophy for malapropism or inarticulate geniuses.) We can learn the technique of logic and of arguing correctly just as we learn to swim and drive. For most of our days we are not even actively engaged; we are just habit-forming animals, passively conditioned by experience. Even the acts of the "mind" which are so effortless as to appear to be intuitive or direct are so only because "a long run of previous efforts has long since inculcated complete facility in making them."

In laying such emphasis on the preponderance of habit and passivity in our daily lives, Ryle makes no reference to a distinction common among medieval philosophers and moralists between acts performed here and now, acts which are habitual and acts which are virtual. They distinguished carefully, moreover, between intellectual habits, such as the habit of charity or prudence, and the psychophysical habits. Again they always asked themselves whether an intention, formed some time ago and never explicitly revised, continues in force. For safety's sake they recommended that an intention should be kept alive by recalling it at intervals.

Such is Ryle's case, and it ought to make us chary of calling for a tune from the mind which it cannot play. But if it be less respectably intellectual than we thought and often only a half-breed, the distinction between the mental and the physical remains as indelible as ever. No more than a mirage is real is the thought of a gold coin the same as a gold coin in nature. Ryle commits the error which Buber so severely condemned of treating a person as a thing. Everything is a piece of goods on a counter, and the observer is on the counter too. This is the mortal sin of the empirical approach, as Merleau-Ponty pointed out. In keeping with the same kind of wrong thinking, Ryle argues that if the self had its own privacy it would be condemned to an "absolute solitude." There could be no communication, for "it would follow that no one has ever yet had the slightest understanding of what anyone else has ever said or done." This is a completely *a priori* dogmatic statement and one made with shut eyes. We have the evidence of our own eyes, material and spiritual, that we live with others, that we share much but not everything, and that it is in fact quite difficult to communicate with some and comparatively easy with others. But when we say "communicate," we do not mean obviously that we or the other persons are open pages to be read. No one in his senses thinks that he understands another completely: he does not completely know himself. So it is that if, instead of dogmatizing without looking, we go by the evidence, we must conclude that human beings are of the sort who have much in common and much that is private. What is really remarkable is something quite different. It is this; that we have private feelings and emotions which are, strictly speaking, inexpressible. Nevertheless, by some kind of conjuring, we are able to make others understand to some extent what we are undergoing. This—and it is a pity Ryle has not reflected on it—is just what the skillful artist does. He defies the skeptic by managing to translate a feeling into language, relying on analogies from the other senses and illuminating images and finally choosing exactly the right words to radiate the truth of what he is describing. But speculations such as Ryle's, important as they were to me as I formed the Credo that is at the core of this book, remained barren and fruitless until they encountered the reality of the person in whom all speculations found reality.

In his book on *Individuals* P. F. Strawson made out a case for the reality of what we call "persons." Persons he argued are more than a string of sensations and memories. They own certain attributes, possess consciousness and feelings, and have individual physical characteristics. So far so good, but innumerable questions pour in. How are the mind and the body in these persons combined? What further characteristics of the self are there for the searching? Is the self a true agent and free, and if so, what kind of subsistence has it? What is the possibility of survival after death? Most of these questions may be beyond the scope of Strawson's book; he does, nevertheless, make some suggestive remarks about the possibility of survival. He argued for a self which satisfied commonsense language, and this self is what we can recognize as embodied mind, a self which in a particular body owns its thoughts and feelings. This conception of the self does not give hope for survival; a disembodied spirit would have no self to own and could not communicate with others.

Strawson may forbid himself any further inquiry into the status of the human self, but the problems which cluster around it are so living and pressing that discussion about them will never cease. A.J. Ayer thinks that there is no principle to rule out the possibility of several selves having identical experiences. There are stories of diabolical possession, cases of split personalities, and remarkable incidents of empathy. But in every example quoted, the continued existence of the original self is presupposed. It is only in our happy possession of imagination that we can play with the idea of selves turning into different persons and enjoy the pictures of centaurs and cunning-tongued serpents and Pucks, Undines and vampires. Can the self which has its own unique experiences continue in any way to enjoy them after death? And when considering this question, we must first omit the Christian doctrine of the resurrection of the body. Strawson maintains that without the body we should cease to be individuals, and without the senses we could not communicate with others. In taking this view, he is not being eccentric, for he is re-echoing a doubt expressed by followers of Aristotle and even of St. Thomas Aquinas. Aristotle looked upon the soul as the animating principle of the body. Wherever there is life, there is a living unity —a body of such a kind as to have a special name—an organism. As there are various forms of organism, vegetable, animal, and human, Aristotle marks off three different animating principles or souls. These animating principles are not to be thought of as something extra, a new reality in addition to the organic unity, throned, so to speak, in it. They describe what the organism is, a body with a life of its own: it is born, matures, and decays; it struggles for existence and passes on its own life to its progeny. As Aristotle believed that there were different species of organisms, he used the word "form" to designate the specific unity, and so the soul is called the form of the human body.

What differentiates the human being, according to Aristotle, is the presence of reason. He defines man as a rational animal. But can a principle which is no more than the life of the body be also the principle of a constituent of the self so different from body as mind is? Some think that Aristotle got out of this difficulty by a special view of his own about what he calls "nous." There is a famous passage about this in the *De Anima* which is much debated. It is not at all clear. He says that the soul is the form of a body which is potentially alive, and, in the case of man, it not only actualizes the various human activities of sensing and locomotion and the impulses, but it has also a special activity of "nous." All the powers of the body are inseparable from it, but "nous" pre-exists and is immortal. It comes from outside and it requires a corresponding spiritual ground or potency upon which to act. Hence we must distinguish the active and the passive "nous." The former is the masculine (this adjective should be noted) element and is immortal: the latter is the passive and it perishes (De Anima 3.5, 430 a.) Whatever Aristotle meant he has left us the old difficulties and he does not appear to take us beyond Strawson's captions on immortality.

St. Thomas was aware of these difficulties and had his way of getting around them. Of this I will treat only in so far as it bears on the development of my philosophy of life, the steps of which I have been trying to give. Despite the dry style of St. Thomas, there was not lacking a splendor of vision. St. Thomas said, following Aristotle, that man by his mind had the prerogative of seeing before and after and also of removing objects from their transient setting and of seeing them absolutely for what they are. Furthermore the human being is self-conscious, and has the capacity of reflecting upon himself and his acts, and so is able to realize how his operations stand in terms of truth and goodness. Such an activity must needs be without a bodily organ commensurate with it. It follows that a being which has a mind stands on the horizon of two worlds and reveals a new order beyond that of the sensible world. In this new order, freedom and the knowledge of nature and the supersensible are possible. Being almost a hybrid, however, composed of mind and body, man is more at ease with sensible reality. He is never "uncumbered" of sense; so he takes time to come to self-knowledge and it is only gradually that he can improve his ideas. What lies beyond this world of ours is seen through the sensible images and with the help of the imagination and analogies of human justice and intellect.

The content of mind is indifferent to time: once true is always true. It is independent, also, of place, for the same truth can shine through a million eyes at once and in different parts of the globe. The mind then does not pass away like the body, and so the question keeps on recurring as to what happens when the self casts its slough?

Does it not lose part of itself and the very part which makes it distinct and individual and recognizable? In dealing with this problem, Aquinas first makes sure of the continuity of spirit. He says that "nothing is destroyed by that which makes its perfection; but the perfection of the human soul consists in a certain withdrawal from the body for the soul is perfected by knowledge and virtue." In saying this, St. Thomas may seem to ignore his own view that man's nature is a composite one and that therefore the knowledge and the virtue ought also to be of the composite. Be this as it may, he is concerned to show that the spirit survives, and he would go on to say that the human spirit is cousin to the pure spirits and by that prerogative like even to God. But he is still faced with the difficulty of saying what kind of being it is which survives. His answer is to the effect that philosophy cannot adequately fill in the picture of the soul's condition after death. He suggests, and the suggestion is illuminating, that what he calls the "commensuration" or inner relatedness of the spiritual form to a particular body will "remain in souls even when the bodies perish" and that certainly "the activities remain which are not exercised through organs, and such are understanding and will." These, however, as they are dependent for their working in this life on memory and images, must pass into a higher stage, and the manner of knowing will be "after the manner of those intelligences that subsist totally apart from bodies, such an angels." "The human soul being on the boundary line between corporeal and incorporeal substances, and dwelling, as it were, on the horizon of time and eternity, approaches the highest by receding from the lowest. Therefore, when it shall be totally severed from the body, it will be perfectly assimilated to the intelligences that subsist apart and will receive their influence in more copious streams."

From this account many might conclude that the original difficulty about the state of the soul after death had been aggravated instead of diminished by the Aristotelian theory of "form." His remark, incidentally, about the soul and body being commensurate holds good independently of any theory of "form," and it answers to human experience. One outstanding advantage of the Aristotelian theory of form is that it gets over the soul-body difficulty. Those who hold it are left quite unperturbed by all the intimacies between mind and body discovered by physiologists. As the soul is the form of the body, this is what is to be expected. Those who belong to the Platonic or Cartesian tradition must be ill at ease with such discoveries. They started with the idea that spirit is all-important and that the body was to be looked upon as a help or an encumbrance, a kind of carapace which could be removed without interference with the "real" self. The Aristotelian and the Thomist start from the other end. They hold that an organism is a live unity, and the form is the word for this specific living thing. Their trouble is to explain and justify the existence in the human being of something which is partly in control of the organism and has operations which are not explicable on a purely bodily principle. The real question with those who start in this way is whether the unmistakable presence of a self, which is self-regarding and free and able to direct its own life by immaterial standards, does not call for a revision of the Aristotelian theory.

The perplexities in, and the answers to, this problem could be illustrated by many of the modern thinkers besides those already quoted. I will mention only two, Martin Heidegger and Merleau-Ponty. What is remarkable is the coincidence of their views with those which artists and writers are forcing upon the attention of the public. "Ever since Courbet," writes Andrew Forge, "the artist himself has been painting's central character." It is a movement that you can follow from Courbet's self-portraits and Daumier's mountebanks to Picasso's drawing of the artist's studio, and this reached its climax in German expressionism. This tradition of self-regard stems of course from the whole question of the artist's sense of identity, his doubts as to who he was and what he was meant to be doing. Sartre is often taken to be the doubting Thomas and the sensitive expression of this mood. Certainly he has sent to the guillotine the goddess of reason worshiped at the French Revolution and he has taken a back-to-the-wall attitude to life. But he owes the deeper elements of his philosophy to Heidegger, and he seems less perceptive and cogent than Merleau-Ponty. Heidegger is a kind of modern Hamlet without his gift of clear speech. Few can be sure of interpreting him aright. What he seems to be saying is that I come to myself in a world; I belong to it so that I cannot free myself from it; and yet I do not belong to it because it is what it is whereas I am only a possibility of being. I am not a part of the world; I have to make myself a part of it, and that I can never do. The world is in itself *en soi;* I am for myself, *pour soi.* This makes me an outsider for, by being conscious and self-conscious, co-existent, I am at a remove from what just happens to be. I have to situate all my experience at the center of my own universe of concern, concern for what I should become and concern with the world into which I am flung. In such a condition, I suffer *angst* and loneliness and am like the wandering Jew. In short, I am a projection, emerging or erupting from the world, i.e., things as they are in themselves; infinite possibilities open out before me, which can never be realized; for like golden boys and girls, we have to die and turn to dust. Our general condition, therefore, according to Heidegger, is *sorge,* concern; for hardly have we recognized that we have the power to look out and see a past on one side and a future on the other and have the freedom to become something, than we also discover death. All that we are at the moment consists in being not tied but free and free in the sense of having ourselves the initiative when facing the future. We cannot leave ourselves as just possibilities; a burden is upon us, and we have to carry it; otherwise we would not be free. Moreover, this burden means bearing other person's burdens. To refuse to take one's part in living is the one great sin; it means that we are unauthentic, not having even the semblance of being real.

With death ending all our hopes of ever achieving a selfhood as substantial as the inanimate world of things around us, Heidegger's philosophy looks like black pessimism. His work, however, is still unfinished, and he has given signs of being able to provide a rescue. His idea of the self is almost like an undivine Dali figure on a cross bent down over the world; it is so attached to this world of time as to live by its concern for it. Some of his disciples have thought that by his interest in what is called the "holy," Heidegger is working his way to a theistic and more cheerful solution. It is true that in his later years he has dwelt on what "the poet names the holy." "Poetical images are 'imaginings' in an unusual sense; not simple fantasies and illusions, but imaginings in the form of revealing messages from the unfamiliar which are read in the face of the familiar. . . . Through such readings, God surprises. In these surprises he reveals his unceasing nearness." The gods now are absent, but perhaps they can be brought nigh.

All the same, what Heidegger means by the "sacred" and by the nearness of the gods is very uncertain. Those who know him best warn us not to take sibylline sayings of his in an orthodox theistic sense. Hence we are not safe in going beyond his early doctrine of the self: that it is a stray bit of reality which is conscious and so for itself that it has the possibility in this freedom of becoming all things. Like the condemned princess in the tower, it can look through the slit for a rescuer, who will never come. The state of the self which he describes as *sorge* or *angst* is not far from that which is recorded in so many literatures and can be described as the sense of human mortality. More metaphysically, it can be called the indigence of our being or our contingence. As such, of course, it provides the groundwork for an argument to the existence of God. Again, he recalls the Gnostic heresy when he implies that the self could never be satisfied unless it were united to the whole. For Heidegger it is the desire of the moth for the flame, for the Gnostic it is the desire of the fragment which is not of this world, to return to its divine home. In using the expression "not of this world," one is also reminded of the words of Christ before Pilate. More real perhaps is the resemblance to Plato. In Plato the soul would flee from its only half-real condition and be assimilated with the highest. Plato believed that this could be accomplished, but Heidegger certainly refuses to believe in the possibility of any such destiny.

Heidegger was of little help to me on this particular point. On other points, however, he proved illuminating. One is his description of the self, poised outside the immense round universe like a tiny fledgling that has broken its shell. But the image hides the discovery made by Heidegger of the really exceptional status of the human self. Being free of the limitations of a thing, it can take an interest in what is around it, see it for what it is. The world is at its feet, and this must mean that the human self has reached a form of life in which it can envisage everything. That is very like what Teilhard de Chardin wrote about the noosphere. At a certain level of evolution, there is a reversal; what had been moving outward now starts moving inward. A plant extends out, the mind takes in and produces within itself a reflection of the external reality outside it. The self is not a thing like the objects around it, and the empiricists are mistaken in treating it as if it were. These objects have no past of which they are aware and no future seen in terms of their present; whereas the human self is released from the limitations of the present. It has a past and that past is present to it, and it is engaged with the future already. That future opens up a world of possibilities, for it lies there before us indeterminate. Hence we are a possible being, able to choose where we shall go and buy the ticket. It would seem then a mistake to look upon Heidegger's human self as static or even as persisting the same amidst change, unless in some mysterious way the being and becoming of a person are one and the same.

The thought of Heidegger remains baffling, but not, I discovered, the thought of the late Merleau-Ponty. He does not waste time wondering whether there is a world and whether there are human beings. (Such philosophical speculation dries up the thought of the Existentialists and the linguistic and analytical philosophers, and I found in them, ultimately, nothing to nourish me.) There is no problem here, he says, for the world is in all our experience, and it precedes scientific investigation of it. So too with reason. All day long, we enjoy and depend upon a network of experiences, and we ourselves are the network of relationships. We do not arrive at our knowledge of reality bit by bit; our experience of it is there from the start, as a swimmer might realize that he was in the water and swimming. What we always do is to ask questions about the world which is already there and already and always apprehended with the senses. When, says Merleau-Ponty, I say *with,* I do not mean that the senses are instrumental in helping me to know; they are not conductors. The answers to our questions are already latent in the landscape. The scientific and empirical approach, valuable as it is for adding to our knowledge, is secondary. Primary knowledge—and by that is meant what necessarily precedes our everyday investigations and enables them to make sense—is seen in what we have to take for granted and exploit all day long. Science tells us of the physical and chemical properties of the stimuli which act upon our sensory apparatus; but it does not include or account for the anger or pain which I read in a face, the kind of talk whose nature I seize in an act of hesitation or reticence. Without the stimuli, no doubt, I would not get these impressions, nor could they be presented. But my mental life is not at the end of a series of shots and impulses, beginning on the skin and reaching to the brain. Mental life extends into human space, and that world of space is made up by those with whom I argue and live, the place where I work, the abode of my happiness. This commonplace experience is the central one; and there are examples here, there, and everywhere of it, in our perception of how near the canvas is underneath the picture, the crumbling cement underneath the building, the tiring actor behind his makeup.

The mind when it attends to something first of all creates for itself a field which can be surveyed and then exploited. In doing this, we articulate what was indeterminate before, and up to a point, we make up the object so as to have it dressed for understanding. That is to say that interest is central in our human attending and intending; we feel that we are on the trail of truth as soon as we apprehend even faintly an immanent sense in what is before us. It is nonsense to suppose that in experience we are brought into contact with some pure or neutral quality. We always invest it with value, and our own body serves as a scout and secretary, for we grasp things first in their meaning for us—and by "us" we mean partly our own body. Our body does more faintly for us what the radar of the bats does for their safety. Merleau-Ponty is here enlarging on what it means to be a *pour soi*. He is attacking the idea that we are cool spectators seeing everything as if it belonged to another world from our own. Philosophy of this kind turns everything, even our own body, into an external thing without an interior, and looks on the self actually as an external spectator or ghostlike subject without any status. In place of this view, he says, we have to rediscover that layer of living experience through and in which other people and other things are first given to us. In other words we must bear in mind how self, others, things came together primordially into our experience. That is the point of using the word *Dasein*.

After reiterating his criticism of the ordinary scientific and psychological explanation of how we encounter reality, he sets us right about our own body. (The function of the body is the key to his position, showing both its strength and weakness.) The generally accepted theory that the body serves as a conductor of impressions from outside is exaggerated and misleading; for the brain acts as a pattern-maker even before this critical stage is reached. The truth of the matter is that I am conscious of the body via the world. The body is the unperceived term in the center of the world towards which all objects turn their faces. It is my body which makes me see a ship approaching with my perspective. My body is the pivot of the world; and in that fact lies the paradox contained in the expression "being-in-the-world." I can do many things: seize on a moment during the day and make it decisive in my life, or ignore a situation which would have changed me. That I can do; but with my body, it is different. It has a prepersonal conformity with the general form of the world and as an anonymous and as a general existence plays below the level of my personal life the part of an inborn complex. Because of this, we are both free and in servitude. Man has a setting and a world of his own. What a man can do is make a space between the world and himself, so that external stimulations impinge upon him "with a bow," and he does not allow any particular situation to be everything in the world to him. He keeps things at a distance, and he keeps a hold upon himself, his personal self. "Thus it is by giving up part of his spontaneity by becoming involved in the world through stable organs and pre-established circuits that man can acquire the mental and practical space which will in his mind liberate him from his environment and allow him to *see* it."

It is as being related to the world in this way through the body and at the same time being apart from it that the self has its first opening upon things, the body not being a mere form. It is more like an attitude towards existence or a possible task. In conformity with this view, we must not look upon the body's spatial contour as one of position; it is rather one of situation. To bring out what he means by this, Merleau-Ponty takes the example of leaning on a table with one's hands. Here one is not unaware of one's shoulders and feet, but they are included in the position of the hands. Again, when we use the word "here," we mean the laying down of the first coordinates, the anchoring of the active body in an object. Bodily or external space is the void in front of which the object, which is the goal of action, can come to light. .Our projects serve to polarize the world, bringing magically into view a host of signs which guide action, as notices in a museum guide a visitor. So it is that in questioning reality and in searching within it, we place beneath the flow of impressions an explanatory invariant and give a form to the stuff of experience. This is the power of consciousness, or rather, let us say more correctly, that this power is consciousness, for consciousness is a pure-meaning-giving act. A consciousness of nothing is unthinkable; it always refers to an object, and in ordinary life it is nothing but a network of intentions. Otherwise it would be just a thing in itself and not for itself.

Proceeding along these close phenomenological lines, Merleau-Ponty concludes that beneath the intelligence, considered as an anonymous function or as a categoric process, a personal core has to be recognized. This is the self's power of existing. There is a "vector mobile" turning like a searchlight in all directions, a power through which we can direct ourselves towards anything inside or outside ourselves and adopt a form of behavior towards the object we meet. Another way he uses to express the nature of the self is this: our conscious life is subtended by an intentional arc which projects around about us our past, our future, our human setting, our physical, ideological, and moral situation; or rather, which results in our being situated in every one of these respects. It brings about the unity of all that is in us, and it goes limp in times of illness. This self forms habits, dilates itself as it proceeds making its human habitation and changes its way of existing by appropriating fresh instruments for its life-needs, as the knowledge in our hands in typing is forthcoming only when needed. We need to correct the conventional view of the body as a physical object; it is more like a work of art, for it is a focal point of living meaning and not the function of a number of mutually variable terms. It is in the world as the heart is in the organism; it keeps the visible spectacle constantly alive; it breathes into it and sustains it inwardly, and with it forms a system. So vital is its work and so dependent on it are we that the philosophers who treat it as a thing in the world to be explained like any other thing go grievously wrong. Our perception is with the body, and all knowledge takes its place within the horizons opened up by perception. It follows that there can be no question of describing perception itself as one of the facts thrown up in the world; we can never, in the picturing of the world, fill up the gap which we ourselves are and by which the world comes into existence for whoever it is, since perception is the flaw in this great demand. It cannot do the double work of perceiving and being the perceived.

It is clear that Merleau-Ponty thinks that the discussion of many of the so-called problems of perception is a waste of time. He says that they belong to our pre-history, meaning by that that there has been an earlier conformity of the body with the world around it. That is exemplified in the way we accept the equivalence of breadth and depth and see a face the right way up instead of upside down. He holds, too, that we have always some kind of an "I" or subject, though he is one who sleeps and forgets himself, wakes and is lost in an absorbing experience. There is always the presumptive unity of the self on the horizon of our experience. We can go further; it is permissible from the evidence of our experience to describe the self as an élan which bears *itself* along, and, moreover, this it cannot do without being aware of this and without drawing itself together in the very same act whereby it bears itself along. When the self looks within, it has a glimpse of an ever-moving stairway, a flux of consciousness which has no qualifications. We encounter limitations, but it is not the "I" which is jealous or hunchbacked or sick. The "I" can pull a snook at such things. Until the final coma, the dying man is inhabited by a consciousness; he is all that he sees and he has always this outlook no matter what the world does to him. Consciousness can never objectify itself into an invalid consciousness or a cripple consciousness; and even if an old man does complain of his age, it is by comparing himself with others and seeing himself through others' eyes or taking a statistical and *objective* view of himself. Each one of us in the depths of his being feels beyond his limitations and as a result submits to them. This is the price paid for being-in-the-world.

Merleau-Ponty sums up his views as follows. "To understand is to bring about here and now the synthesis of the object and because we live in our perceptions and through the body, the thing always has a significance for us. . . . But when I understand, it is not I who here and now effect this synthesis. I come to it (as to a picture) bringing my sensory fields and my perceptual field with me and, in the last resort, I bring a schema of all possible being or universal setting in relation to the world. As then the world is at the heart of the subject himself, he is not precisely synthetic activity; man is an *ek-stase,* and all that we do when signifying, all our acts too of positive intentionality have beneath them something which is the condition of their possibility; that is to say, an operative intentionality already at work before any positing or any judgment. This is what Husserl called a 'Logos of the aesthetic world,' an art hidden in the depth of the human soul, one which, like any art, is known only by its results."

Merleau-Ponty gathers up into his theory of perception and of the life of man so many of the ideas which have been snowballing in the preceding pages that it might be surmised that I think his solution or synthesis is the right one. If it were not for my great respect for him, I would say that he is like Lucifer, the great pretender to the kingdom of truth. He shakes the past into shape, getting rid of false problems and marking down the power of the self to make a synthesis. He shows us how the self is an *ek-stase* and while of this world it is nevertheless not of this world; he emphasizes the role of the body, and then, when all looks well, he lets us down completely with his existentialist sense of doom and allowing that death has the victory. Death stops him in his tracks and he seems to hear the muffled drums of the Existentialists. This pessimistic note pervades so many of the Existentialists; there is always in their thought the sound of the ferryman's oar. Merleau-Ponty clings fast to the assumption of being-in-the-world, and so, being a creature of time, he rejects theism. The self is made to tick off the hours like a clock and run down, and at the same time it is able to count the hours and explain the mechanism. "We are nothing but a view of the world," he tells us, and this view is given to us by the body which is connatural with other things. Even our interpretation or understanding of the world, which looked so enlightening, is a body-view, whatever that means. But I am thankful to him for showing me the intimate connection of our body with the world in which we live. If we allow that the body does make us one with the world around us, but at the same time allow for the possibility of transcending its limitations, we may both come nearer the full significance of Merleau-Ponty's suggestion and be more faithful to his own inspiration than he is himself. The flaw in his thought is that he has not realized that we are on the horizon of two worlds and that all our development, as I hope to show, is not towards extinction, but a preparation for a new birth.*

Our human self is an élan, a flux which itself performs the movement; it is that "pitch" of being which is the core of our being, the *ek-stase* which gathers what is outgoing and looks to what is incoming. But there is a strange quality about the self described by Merleau-Ponty which chimes with so much that philosophers from the earliest times have been compelled to say. This quality can be summed up in the statement that the self seems to have deep roots but remains curiously anonymous, a lost child who does not know its family or its name. Eastern philosophies look to a complete transformation; Heraclitus was struck by its kaleidoscopic nature—all is change, like fire which is never the same. Plato felt that the truth could

---

* In an essay on *The Structure of Consciousness,* Michael Polanyi has some acute and valuable comments on this shortcoming of Merleau-Ponty.

never be found in this world of images; Aristotle has left us in doubt as to the nature of the individual. Kant fell back on postulates after he had reduced the self to a subject without content. Hegel was convinced that subject and object were in opposition to each other and that we had best regard the self as estranged from itself, and history showed the gradual reconciliation. Marx used the same language at first, saying that man when he became a worker became at the same time estranged from himself, seeing himself as an object and as a worker. This very estrangement does, however, serve the purpose of making him conscious of being a man, though at first he gives himself a false personality and creates a world of religion. Finally, we have the Existentialists with their distinction, succinctly put by Sartre in terms of *en soi* and *pour soi.* The self now is a possibility moving with a dynamic intensity to make itself real and never succeeding. Adam and Eve are out of their Paradise, estranged from Him who is, and so from themselves. They named the creatures of God in Eden, but now they cannot even give themselves a proper name.

The position I have reached so far, in this explanation of my Credo, seems to me to benefit by a reminder of Hopkins' "infinitesimal positive" and his "freedom of pitch." Here, if we remember, lay the secret of the individual personality of each human being. To give an image concordant with the language of Merleau-Ponty, this self is like the conductor of an orchestra. That is to say, he makes the sense come out of the music, but at the same time no two conductors ever give the same identical interpretation. It will also be noticed that freedom comes into these interpretations. Hopkins called the self "freedom of pitch." The image of the conductor on the stage is, therefore, of help, and perhaps even more that of the actor. The actor plays a part and should be wholly in the part. For him aesthetically, while he is on the stage, there is nothing else. Now our public life, which is partly determined for us by needs, education, and pressures, and partly freely chosen, is also a part which we have to live, and we are immersed in it, but not wholly. There have been cases of split-personalities, of dissociation such that a man takes up an entirely new character and form of living, oblivious of what he was before. On Hopkins view he is the same man as before; it is the same "self," but he is like an Athenian who has now a Sparta to adorn. There are, too, the Jekyll and Hyde types who keep a foot in both camps. These changes are for the most part abnormalities and exhibit an impoverished life; it is a case of loss and not of mutation. A simple and clear case is that of the man who by effort of will has increased his virtues and grown by action in sympathy and generosity even to a heroic degree; suppose that through an operation on the brain or a disturbance of the genes he turns into a complaining sourpuss or into an uncaring blockhead. The correct answer here is that the man is no longer fully responsible, but in so far as he is, whatever belonged to the original and creative self and could be said positively to be his, such as free loving actions, are written into his self and remain there forever.

To use again the language of Hopkins, the self as freedom of pitch needs a field of play and of exercise in which it can recognize itself and be recognized. Without such a field, and let us call it a theistic philosophy, the self is defenseless and uncertain of its rights and aims. This is a radical uncertainty and not to be confused with private and accidental alarms and worries, which of course may perchance be connected with it. How we look out upon the world and our neighbors is partly determined by childhood impressions and by what we are told by our elders. We probably pass through, most of us, a phase of co-consciousness like to that of the primitives, who extrapolate their inner lives in that of the tribe or village or community. There is such an abundance of evidence showing that boys and girls, when translated from the routine conventions of home life, can go quite astray, ignore what they should be, and play the fool. Again, there will always be with us some who, for one reason or another, lack self-confidence and hold on to apron strings, or, on the contrary, have such a conceit of themselves that they act as if indifferent to public opinion and do just as they please. They are like "Old Talbot's ghost, he speaks with such a grand, commanding spirit." Then there are the young who have to learn their capacities and weaknesses by experience in competition and by "facing reality." As their powers are still immature and their growth depends partly on their own decisions, they are in self-protection shy and they tend to wear a mask.

These are all variations on the radical condition of the self when it has to make its way and discover itself in the course of living. By this I do not mean that we do not have everyday certainties both about the world around us and about ourselves. Cook Wilson has made this plain, but, as already indicated, we can know much and yet be persecuted by the thought that it is all illusion and that there is no meaning to life. Almost every week in magazine or newspaper one will find a statement such as this: "There is a horror in things, a horror at heart of the meaninglessness of existence" (Tennessee Williams); or the remark of a Birmingham girl: "You turn a corner—

it could be something beautiful or it could be a cliff edge." Here is put startlingly the difference between what I called earlier the distinction between the certain and the true, between what I happen to be sure of and my trust in the universe at large. Georges Poulet in his *Studies in Human Time* says that the gap between these two widens when God is not there to pull everything together. I say that I am certain that I am trying to tell the truth—but what is the truth? I have an innate respect for a person or I may be in love with another and everything I read tells me that these persons are animals without free will or bundles of sense data or complicated organisms or *pour sois* which have no *en soi* reality. Why then should I continue to do what I am certain is right? Even my own self starts before my very eyes to do a disappearing trick, as if I were worse than a gorgon. Unless I can make sense of the world about me and of myself, am I not forced to say that even my certainties are ultimately without meaning? All is silent: there is no answer to my questions, and if they were forthcoming, I might not be there to receive them. I am like the sea captain in Dostoevsky's *The Possessed*. Shatov had just said that if a revolution should start in Russia, it will have to start with the promulgation of atheism. "An old tough sea captain, with grey hair, sat and sat in silence and did not breathe a word. All of a sudden he rose in the very middle of the room and, you know, said aloud just as if speaking to himself: 'If there is no God, how can I then be a captain?' He took his cap, threw up his hands, and left."

The two requisites for self-knowledge and for the sense of general well-being are, first, the belief which gives a meaning and destiny to the individual, and, secondly, the corroboration of our self-knowledge in the sympathetic understanding of us by others. In some respects this double need corresponds with the distinction, already made, between Eros and Agape, centripetal and centrifugal love. The self requires that kind of wisdom which insures its independence and freedom. I am what I am by God's bounty, and my decisions are "doing-be's" of the sort in which I commit myself, and I take my life in my hands. Such independence does not entail a high idea of oneself. It is rather the outcome of Oxford's motto *Dominus Illuminatio Mea,* "The Lord is my light whom then shall I fear?" We can however fear ourselves, and it is in the companionship of friends that we expand and in true love that we forget our fears and fancies. A theistic philsophy, therefore, and a co-conscious life of mutual affection are the best guarantee of the self's well-being.

In descriptions of the self, I have made use of the image "playing a part." This was natural and convenient because in both Latin and Greek the words for a person are "persona" and "prosopon," and they mean literally a mask or taking a part. The tradition of this still lingers in the theaters, where the programs contain the "dramatis personae," the names of the characters in the play. Much has been written by scholars about the connection in early times between religious festivals and plays, and it has been held that the theater developed out of the religious rite. Tribal consciousness was overwhelmingly strong amongst the primitives, so that their life could be described as a co-conscious one, and this came out especially in the religious ceremonies. One of the chief characteristics of these ceremonies consisted in putting on masks. They dressed up (and this was part of the mask), painted themselves, and put on head-masks; they then carried out the rite, singing and dancing until they passed into a trance or collapsed. Behind the ceremeony was the belief that in it they entered into a closer unity with the spirit or daimon or god of the tribe; they took on his power and character, and the mask was the symbol of this union and the very enactment of it. They played the part of the mask, and this mask represented their god; thus they put on their god. As religion threw off its swaddling clothes and became more mature, it kept the numinous element present in the first, primitive rituals. The animistic or magical accompaniments decreased, and a higher conception of the deity developed. By degrees, the individuals of the tribe became more self-conscious and independent and, parallel with this went higher forms of worship. Of God and the evidence for Him this is not the occasion to write. For the moment we are concentrating on man, on man as a person and his relationship with God. Without God, it has been suggested that the figure of man looks as incomplete as a pain without a background. Some years ago there appeared in a reputable magazine an account of a young man in South Africa who had the gift of water-divining. He discovered after a time that he could save himself making long journeys to places where farmers wanted to use his gifts by staying at home and using a map. Held over a map, the hazel-stick performed in the same way in which it did where water was to be found below the soil. Now the evidence for this seemed unimpeachable, and yet it did not seem to make sense, no more than that some persons, while blindfolded, can read with their chins. . . . My point is that to many now, as in the past, this world, in the absence of God, does not make sense. No doubt many will immediately reply that the findings of modern science and philosophy do make sense. Let us grant that the scientists within their own field can be happy and may be impeccable; but we have already seen the traps into which they have fallen, and I need not repeat the quotations from Haldane and C.S. Lewis to indicate what is meant. It will be better to try and exhibit this relationship of the self to God and show that it is needed if man is to be seen full-faced.

If there be a God, and if what is presupposed in the language about Him and in the forms which worship takes be true of Him, then the relationship between the self and God must be so intimate and so special as to defy a fully adequate description. The theologian who is relying on reason and not on the help given by the Christian revelation is forced back on general terms which hold for all existent relationships, terms such as cause, necessity, existence. They carry the mind along, but only as heavy oars can move a speedboat. A less metaphysical or logical way might be to lay out for all to see by illustration what this relationship involves. Words like cause and contingency and effect are so common in our experience; they are used for public and private occasions, for turning on the gas, consuming food, writing books, and improving the birthrate. As a result we feel that they fall deplorably short of what we want to say when we pray to God as the sustainer of life, as providence and as lover of the self, this God "in whom we live and have our being." If we are so bound up with Him that we cannot do without Him, then by examining the experience of those who deny God in their lives or the generations which subsist on secular principles, we may be able to discern more vividly the nature of this relationship. When the idea and significance of God slip from the mind, and no one bothers about His judgments or Providence, there ensues perhaps at first a sense of release and independence; but there follows the danger of man overreaching himself. We have either the Miles Gloriosus or the first feeling of a Faust at having made a good bargain with the devil. Even at the beginning, however, as Georges Poulet points out, a sense of insecurity makes itself felt, the same kind of feeling which primitive man had when changing his haunts. Death is no longer the gate to life; it is the end; and nature, too, has a face averted or like a faun can look one moment pleasant and the next frightening and cruel. The state of man without God peers through the literature of Israel, even though they enjoyed God's special protection. Their sin makes them realize what they are missing, and so the Psalms continually make moving appeals to God that he should be to them as of old: "See if on any false paths my heart is set, and thyself lead me in the ways of old." The gods are absent, says Heiddegger; it is the twilight of the gods. Rather he should have said that it is the night of the self; for now it doubts its own reality; it may be just a piece of nature, the flotsam and jetsam of nature's high tides, or possibly a part of a greater whole, seed lost in the furrow before a universal harvesting. Anything may happen. If we are to trust Nietzsche, certainly nothing happy, for to judge by him, man wants God back. "Man has attempted to do without God. What then? Whither does the earth now move? Whither do we ourselves move? Away from every sun? Are we not constantly falling? Are we not groping our way in an infinite nothingness? Do we not feel the breath of the empty spaces? Has it not become colder? Is there not night, and ever more night?"

Nietzsche's cry may be that of a poet and a sick man. Nevertheless, there is plenty of corroboration that Cain is the symbol of man without God. "Cain at his orisons, Narcissus at the mirror." A murderer detained at Alcatraz wrote a poem called "The Egotist." It ran: "I looked in the mirror, gee! It's me!"—Cain and then the Narcissus self gazing into a blurred mirror and dissatisfied with the sight. Pasternak, living where orisons were not easy, is another witness. In *Dr. Zhivago* he makes one of his characters say that "the whole human way of life has been destroyed and ruined. All that is left is the naked human soul stripped to the last shred . . . shivering and reaching out to its nearest neighbor as cold and as lonely as itself. . . . It is in memory of all those vanished wonders that we live and love and weep and cling to one another." This sense of loneliness is pervasive in so much modern literature, and it is backed by the Existentialist philosophy, where the self is an excrescence.

But before this idea could be worked out, I had to learn more about my *self*. It was necessary to bring into order the various clues given by Hopkins' freedom of pitch, field and exercise and Merleau-Ponty's élan, the river which bears itself along. We are in the world, I discovered, like a bee in a hive, and so I must not shirk its burdens or turn my back upon it. If I face reality and am faithful in playing my part in it, I shall encounter other persons like myself and meet them as persons. A dialogue will ensue, and the world will become more and more open and enlist my faith in it. But my faith will not stop at the world; it will pass over to the presence of its creator, God. In this act I realize that "we are not our own masterpieces," "what is deepest in me is not of me."

This cosmic view which makes up one's faith allows for that individualism, the freedom of pitch, which is the very core of human personality. We can see the sharp differences within a common background of the three leading Greek dramatists; we could not mistake the work of

Shakespeare for that of Dante. The Phenomenologists have dug up from the human consciousness a primordial way of seeing the universe, which anticipates conscious judgments; the world exists in my life before I make it an object of thought, and my organs of contact with the world bear the traces of it. I would not be a human being with a body formed out of the world I see, were this not the case. My own unique and very personal way of interpreting the universe is conditioned by this antecedent primary cohabitation with nature. Now if I curtail my own vision so as to ignore the hinge or axis on which all turns, namely God, my ideas fall apart or form a new artificial unity; or to change the image, like a plant without water, I may sicken and die. Such is the relationship that we cannot do without what Farrer calls subjectively "aspiration" and Kierkegaard and Nietzsche and Heidegger call the idea of the Holy or God. Our nature is such that this is bound to be so. We have connaturality with the universe and aspiration, and either way God stands at the beginning and the end. Through connaturality, we are able to find out something about nature and also something about ourselves. Behind the simplest act of knowing is this desire to know nature, ourselves and God; what is not ourselves, our own true name and what gives meaning and worthwhileness to all our pursuits. We are back again at the distinction of *pour soi* and *en soi* and the Pascalian truth that we are always searching for what we have already found. In the language of love, this comes to saying that we find ourselves fully at home with nature and with ourselves when we recognize ourselves and all else in the divine creative act of God. At that point *Eros,* the self-developing and self-asserting principle must yield finally to *Agape*. In the early religions there is a ritual performance, and in some of the early but great philosophies there is a word, which are both revealing. The word is "assimilation" (v. Gospel, "likening oneself"), and it represents the constant effort of man to assimilate himself to what is highest in thought and imagination. It is precisely in the ritual performance that we see him putting this desire and hope into action. The rite is marked by the wearing of the god's mask, and by so dancing and chanting that the self is carried out of self-consciousness into the rhythm and life of the god. When man had attained the stage of full rational life, this communal act of the rite was superseded by more individual aspirations, and these aspirations revealed themselves in two conflicting movements, the one which can be called Promethean, and the other Dionysiac. The rational self seeks a perfection, but by developing its own powers and its own freedom of judgment and conscience. By this ingrowing activity, it realizes itself in part, but all the time it is aware of a stronger pull—to go beyond itself and find another. Finally there is the soul's demand that the two should come together in one great love or form of happiness. The mystics show one way, and dreamers conceive of utopias. Still another has been attempted by P. Teilhard de Chardin. He has the strong hope that a time will come when, without any loss of personalities, mankind by thinking alike in truth about universal peace and concord will reach one chorus of love and knowledge in Him who is Alpha and Omega.

VI

MASKS OF GOD

THE VARIOUS IDEAS assembled up to now, in this description of my odyssey toward a Credo, can best be seen in their unity in the language of the mask. On a first impression, philosophy and theology may not appear to have much in common with masks. The capital importance of the mask comes from this—that it has from time immemorial been the active manner in which man has chosen to hide and so to reveal himself and act out his ideals. The mask serves, as nothing else can, to reveal a man's identity and also his relation with God. My problem was always to answer this question: "Who am I?" the key question, as Wallace Fowlie believes, in all aspects of Modernism, whether it be Surrealism or Existentialism, as opposed to the key question of the preceding age, "What shall I do?" Melville's writings, again, are said to be "dramatic representations of the encounter of the self and nonself, of the single human person and all that is set over against him, the total reality of nature, mankind, and God." Yeats, as is well known, was fascinated by the secret of the mask when he learnt of its use in the Noh plays of Japan, and he became convinced that "we are all on a public stage, making faces or wearing masks."

Within recent years anthropologists have devoted much attention to masks, and specimens have been gathered in collections from all parts of the world. They go back to the beginning of history and before. In the cave of Trois Frères at Amiége in France, we can still see the figure of a dancing man on the wall, and his head has a covering resembling a deer's head. Scattered about in museums, there are now a vast variety of masks worn by Eskimos, Maoris, natives of New Guinea, Pre-Columbians, Huron and Iroquois, natives of the Gold Coast, the Belgian Congo, Northern Rhodesia, and Navaho Indians. Masks therefore, it can truly be said, are intimately associated with the development of man. Their uses, of course, have been varied; they can serve to hide and to conceal or protect, like gas-masks during the First World War; or, again, they are worn as a decoration and for solemn occasions and rites. Another function is that of a magical weapon to weaken and master the strange inhuman powers of nature that threaten man.

Connected with this, but more important, is its value as a form of impersonation. Ancestors, for example, are impersonated so that they might continue to live on in their living descendants. Most significant of all is the impersonation of these dead or of the gods. A son could by means of such impersonation become the living incarnation of his father or of the hero of the family. Similarly, by playing the part of the spirit of the tribe or the god, whether in primitive rites or in the mystery religions, the initiate was united with the divinity. This change over of personality, the transition from the profane to the sacred, usually took place in secret ceremonies and in the dark and after a long preparation. But it also took place in the sacred dances and with the wearing of special masks, the mask denoting the metamorphosis. A modern light version of these old practices and beliefs is to be found in Max Beerbohm's story of the *Happy Hypocrite*. Here a Lord George Hell, having fallen in love with a pure and innocent girl, woos her under the mask of a saint and under the name of Lord George Hill. The moral of this story is that if we pretend to be what we are not and assume characters and act them, we may come after a while to be unsure who we are, whether we are our old self or the new self we have been "sporting." In Beerbohm's story much depends upon the use of the name. The name in some mysterious way is the person. In old tales a secret self is often presupposed, a self with a secret name or hidden identity. This precious identity could be thought of as the soul or the heart. When an enemy was slain, his heart might be torn out and with its loss and the loss of the blood, there was no chance, it was felt, of the enemy returning to work any more mischief. Even after a clearer idea of the self had developed, a belief in a household or family genius continued, and a genius like Julius Caesar could believe in his "fortune." This is not unlike the belief in the tutelary god or daimon. Ulysses was given strength and grace by his patron goddess. Such men usually feel that they have a part to play in an immense drama, and they have to watch out lest they be tricked into swerving from the path destiny has marked out for them. Writers like Heidegger and Sartre lay great stress on being what they call "authentic"; they think that it is all too easy to assume a character and be a sham or a playboy. On the other hand, Huizinga claims in his *Homo Ludens* that simple people like the savages know "nothing of the conceptual distinction between 'being' and 'playing'; he knows nothing of 'identity,' 'image,' or 'symbol' . . . In play as we conceive it, the distinction between belief and make-believe breaks down." He adds that the concept of play merges quite naturally with that of holiness.

The Eskimos provide a good example of the use and importance of the mask. They do not use images; in place of them, they impersonate their gods by painting themselves or dressing up. The favorite means, however, is impersonation by the mask. In their traditional beliefs all animated things had a dual existence; they could at will assume a human or an animal form. When an animal wished to become human, it raised its forearm or wing and pushed up its muzzle or its beak, as if it were a mask; and so it became human. The human form represents the thinking parts of the creature, and at death it becomes a shade. Their custom, consequently, was to make for themselves various kinds of masks, which were kept after death by their kinfolk; they were considered sacred and used at feasts. Divinity resided in them, and the men of the tribe invoked the masks and thanked them. The wearer believes that he is transformed into the kind of being or god it represents.

No doubt, owing to their ignorance, primitive peoples were forced to invent what might be called safety belts as they moved about; they must have felt as we would feel if we were walking in the dark on ground with live wires. They did not know the causes of diseases, nor could they, except by experience, discriminate between what was harmless and what was harmful in nature. Religion, mixed with superstition and magic, was their one resource. Masks played a part in this struggle with nature. The tribe would try to fight off the hostile spirits by putting spells on them or by impersonating them; or they could impersonate their own god and so assume his strength and virtue. It would be in the rituals and in the dance that they could best accomplish this impersonation for, apart from the magic, it was in the masked dance that the emotions mounted, self-control lessened, and trances could be induced. When the early rituals had expanded into the drama of the theater, the mask still continued to be used; it served as an amplifier in a vast open theater and also exaggerated the features of the *dramatis personae*. But there remained other and deeper reasons for its persistence; the old religion was not dead, and the spiritual aspiration had grown even stronger. The connection between the Greek drama and the Eleusinian mysteries is evidence for this, especially after the advent of the Dionysiac cult. In their fears and aspirations, men and women appear to be alike in no matter what part of the world. There is something common between the use of the masks in the Greek drama and in the Japanese Noh plays, the Lion dance in China, and in the dressing up in Tibet, Ceylon and Melanesia. So strong, however, was the force of Christian doctrine in the west that the original, important function of the mask was forgotten; it was looked upon as a relic of the past or a crude anticipation of the vestments put on by bishops and priests and the robes worn at coronations or even of the liturgical rites. Science too had to have its say about the childish superstitions imbedded in the tomfoolery of the mask; and so for the last few centuries, masks have been reserved for comedies or trivial occasions, the domino at the ball or the disguise of the fair lady hiding her charms as the moon hides behind clouds.

Once more, however, interest has revived as we have come at last to realize that man does not live by the bread of reason alone. Amongst the Existentialists, reason has abdicated, and in the English-speaking world logic has become the supreme interest. The Existentialists are therefore in a better way to welcome the other activities of the self, and in the world of letters and among the more humane sciences, such as anthropology, much more attention is being given to the work of the imagination and the place of symbols and of myths in the expression of truths. Myths are no longer despised as childish fancies; they are taken to be the dramatic representations of some of the deepest experiences of the soul. Jung contributed greatly to the new understanding of the famous myths of the past. He brought his generation back to an awareness of the subliminal world of the self with what may be its race consciousness and ghost voices. Mircea Eliade has complemented the work of Jung by his detailed account of the rich complexity of primitive religion. The easy way of summing it up as magic and superstition has now been discarded; the evidence multiplies to show that early man possessed an almost mystical feeling for the unity of all life. This went with a supernormal sensitivity which enabled these primitive artists to create works of art which not only show a strange empathy with other living things but have as well a paranormal religious intensity. They clearly believed in a supernatural world, a paradise which they felt was so near and yet invisible. It was almost a question of "turn but a stone and touch a wing." As with the more developed religions, they were vividly conscious of sin, they were transfixed by the "numinous," and they were sure that the sacred was their true atmosphere. As their religion was more instinctive than reflective, it pivoted on good behavior, on the beneficial or harmful effect of the spoken word, and on the act duly and ritually performed. Done correctly, the act took on a kind of sacramental character. In the ceremonies it did what it mimed, and so produced what it signified. To put on the mask of the god and to perform the steps of the dance ceremoniously spelled participation in the divine power. The mask served to betoken what the tribe or the individual hoped to achieve or be. Naturally in the higher religions the sense of self and the awe of God are more highly developed; and so the gods must be approached after preparatory rites of purification and in silence. Before the gods, man is as nothing; his very existence depends on their goodwill; so it is possible that amongst the wise as amongst the simple, there is always an undercurrent of fear that the play may be for nothing. *Ex umbris et imaginibus in veritatem,* "out of the shadows and the pageantry of images unto truth"; these scriptural words chosen by Newman for his motto need only a slight change of "masks" for "images" to describe the condition of man who never knows who he is.

The mask had much to tell me of man's superstitions, beliefs, and aspirations. I grew to see man at play, dramatizing himself to himself and before others, and impersonating what he fears or holds dear and would like to be. Though we know little or nothing of many of the ancient tribes and peoples, we have a clue to them, their habits, beliefs, and nature by examining the masks which they wore. These masks form a bridge over the centuries; they show us how repetitive and alike man's habits are. Is it not striking that we can compare masks from modern Mexico and South America with pre-Christian forms, and then make another comparison with what modern artists, like Max Ernst, Cirico, and Picasso, do? In some ways masks are even more revealing than speech or writing.

They are like a magic mirror which shows what a man looks like to himself and to others, and in what direction his fears and desires lie. Thought is often merely a reflection on a deed already over and done with; the mask is the very action or drama itself speaking. Language, it has been said, serves to hide as much as to reveal. Exaggerated though this be, for truth must come to us by word and hearing, the ordinary man now can be all too often confused by technical jargon, and in the labyrinth of ideas lose his direction and proper sense of himself. So it is that the mask can let us into secrets which were otherwise hidden; we catch man confessing in his act what he feels himself to be and what he is trying to be. He is always a *homo ludens*, whereas he is a *homo rationalis* sometimes only in name.

Homo ludens was the title Huizinga gave to a work of originality. The description calls up before the mind numerous images: foxes at play, birds wheeling in the air, Bali dances, Olympic games, Columbine and Harlequin, Degas figures, and the speech in the *Book of Wisdom*: "I was at his side, a master workman, my delight increasing each day, as I made play before him all the while; made play in the world of dust, with the sons of Adam for my playfellows." Man as dramatic, especially in a tragic role, is an image easily recognized today. He is not a "thinking reed," but a reed shaken by every wind. It is idle, therefore, to say "I think, therefore I am," and sit back; it is my unexplained existence which cries out for explanation. Man begins with being-in-the-world and looks around with "concern"; then, after thrashing around like a fish on a hook, he is overcome with nausea. Sartre describes this in a scene from his *La Nausée*. His character Roquentin wears a mask; he is sitting in the park and as he looks down at the twisted roots of a tree beside him, he is revolted and filled with nausea. Behavior serves as an indication of our intention and ideas. Professor Gilbert Ryle would go further and stake all on behavior. So, too, Wittgenstein in his later work took games as having affinities with the way we use words, as if to play were the most revealing action of all men. But I doubt if a study of masks would bear them out; half the way, perhaps, but not all the way. Better to turn to the poets, to men like Yeats who was so sensitive to the purpose of masks. He found within himself so many idols, each of which purported to be his real self. He was confused with this cloud of witnesses, the while he watched himself with a certain derision playing different parts in public, some of which caused him jubilation and others shame. True life, he decided, must consist of some form of impersonation, the putting on of another self, what Oscar Wilde called the making of oneself into a poem. More realistic, Yeats declared: "I think that all happiness depends on the energy to assume the mask of some other self; that all joyous and creative life is a rebirth as something not oneself." Berenson, too, perhaps because he spent so much of his time among creations of art or because of the startling changes in his own fortunes, felt at one time in accord with Yeats's diagnosis of the self. The self we keep in stock, he said, was only an "image to which others approach as to a trading post in old China"; and he came at one period to think of a complete life as an "ending in so full an identification with the not-self that there is no self left to die."

Old tales, perhaps, contain more wisdom than the opinions of the individual artists, and the story of *Beauty and the Beast* might be almost a comment written on masks.

The beast, it will be remembered, had been human, but is under a spell or a curse and so has to wear the mask of a beast. He is not fated to live in such a plight forever for the love of some pure person, Prince or Princess, can restore him to his proper shape. In other tales man is depicted as seeing himself as the Fool or Simpleton, the Pierrot or Harlequin; he dreams of a lost paradise and stretches his arms out in longing for a further shore. There are masks which show him as prince or beggar; there are masks of heroes and demigods which he puts on in the beseeching hope that by this act he may join their company. The mask as a transformer goes back to earliest times when almost all that we know of man is contained in the representation of him hunting, dancing, and masquerading. The evidence when put together suggests that, mask or no mask, he found out certain ways of putting on divinity or a higher self. He practiced rhythms of breathing and self-control, techniques of posture, forms of Hatha Yoga. In Siberia and in the Near East, Shamans imitated the cries of birds and beasts in the conviction that by so doing they could share in the primitive innocence of bird or beast, share, that is, in their paradisiacal state. This is very different from the more modern habit of masquerading, though there is a common ground. We are more complex now and have many faces, the face the family knows and the one at the office, our platform look and the face we wear at the club or pub. Lucky Jims gaze into mirrors, making grimaces to try them out. Such masks are not unlike uniforms or assumed names. Then there is our baptismal, our confirmation name, and the different nicknames at school and among our friends and enemies. "What is in a name?" they say, but when we see our name in print, we do not think this. In fact all seems to be in the name, as the Bible suggests both in the *Apocalypse* and in the Book of *Genesis* when Adam named all living creatures. Hilaire Belloc meant this intimate but revealing name when he wrote of "that great word which every man gave God before his life began"; and it is this word or name which "made God smile when it was shown unforfeited before the throne." Man is always being teased by the cloudy vision of his integrated self, and he hopes for a moment when the mask will have done its work of transformation. He then will have become what he has impersonated, and if that impersonation be a likening to God, he will join the circle of the dancers whom Dante saw in Paradise; the perfect ones wheeling and singing in the presence of Love.

Masks, then, when viewed from outside, are a kind of shop window displaying the fears and hates and likes of mankind. They tell us of human reactions and attitudes to the momentous moments of human life from birth onwards through puberty, at marriage, in community life and at home, in religious crises and at death. What is more, a philosopher would be well advised to inquire into their significance for the mask is a telltale. At first glance it seems designed to hide more than to reveal. It is used, let us grant, to safeguard life; but once the secret signs have been learned and the open sesame spoken, it gives us entry into the sanctuary of the self, where logic cannot penetrate. No tomb of Tutankhamen can compare with the treasures to be found in the self. Conservative-minded people pooh-pooh all this on the grounds that our ordinary experience of the self suffices; but this will not do. Think of the mistakes they make about themselves and about their neighbors. They have not paid sufficient heed to what is implied in the writings of Ibsen and Sartre, Dostoevsky, Freud and Jung, and the evidence they give of fractured and hidden selves. Everything that has preceded this exposition of the function of masks pointed to the need of a philosophy of life which accepted a many-layered self. The mask fits in with and completes the story of man, his needs and his relationship with God. It helps to explain why and how we are at variance with ourselves. There is the self of high or low pitch working through a material which may be inferior or good; it gradually establishes its own personality, and the chief way it does this is by assimilating itself to some ideal or person. This assimilation takes on a dramatic character; we perform and we perform best when there is sympathetic understanding. A philosophy must be lived, and in a living system, the parts which give us here and now our certainties must be such as to cover human experience and at the same time make it harmonious. Limited by a small experience, the dancer with the mask depicted on the early caves was living subconsciously such an authentic life. It should be the same today, despite or with the privilege of a much richer experience: man dancing, behaving, and betraying in such manner a secret hope that he may be like to God and finding his name and destiny written in the Book of Life. Instinctively at first, and later with more intellectual appreciation, man has known that only God can implement and crown his aspirations. Hence it is in religion, as the universality of religion and religious drama bears witness, that man is most committed, has "ultimate concern," and is exposed for what he is. The Christians, so far from quarreling with this, can quote Scripture to confirm it. In the first episode of the Bible, the devil is made to appear masked as a serpent; and the high point of Biblical history is the advent of God in the "form of a man." The disciples are bidden to imitate their Master; as he made himself a Son of Man, so they, by the power of the Cross, are to become the Sons of God, and in and through Christ are to "share in the divine nature." St. Paul and St. John bring the story of the "good news" of Christ to an end in the language of masks. St. Paul demanded of his converts that they should "put on" Christ; St. John promised the Christians of Pergamum that he would give them a "white pebble" and on this pebble or medallion there would be a new name written, which no one will know except God and the recipient of it. The new name is the real self transformed into Christ. The convert is impersonating Christ and wears his mask, and now "Christ plays in ten thousand places, lovely in limbs and lovely in eyes not his to the Father through the features of men's faces."

VII

SUBSTANCE OF THINGS HOPED FOR

"THE WHOLE of our tasks, brethren, in this life consists in healing the heart's eye, through which God is seen." St. Augustine would be the last to play down the part of intellect in faith, but in this passage he gives the last word to love. My Credo as a Christian can but reiterate this saying: I must show how the truths I have experienced or perceived or inferred acquire a new and richer significance. I find the Christian faith to be a form of interpretation, which brings to a head or new unity what I had been sympathetically understanding. With this new understanding, it is possible to go on to a cosmic view of life and to a philosophy which can be lived. Not only, in fact, is this possible, but I should say it is implicit in the act and habit of faith; all that is wanting is the ability and knowledge to articulate it. The act of faith itself is a way of knowing; indeed, it is a very paradigm of knowing. It can come suddenly or after a long maturation; suddenly, as when one says of an acquaintance: "He is really what he claims to be" or "I am now quite sure that he is honest." More commonly, a short or long process precedes the illumination which prompts the act of faith. To take examples from the New

Testament: in the case of St. Paul, the gift of faith was instantaneous; in that of Nicodemus, long pondering was needed; and St. Thomas seemed to have lost his faith and to have recovered it at the sight of the wounded hands. Diverse as such an act may seem from the deciphering of a code or the meaning of an unseen in a foreign language, the discovery of a joke or the sense of Kant's Transcendental Deductions or the grave quality of Bach's music, they are all of the same stock. They are all examples of the power of the mind to interpret or divine a meaning in what are signs or clues. Some of these are clearer cases of intellectual effort or sagacity than others, but I have jumbled them together purposely because, when together, it is easier to see that they are all, in different degrees, acts of cognition. In many cases of belief we can be mistaken, but there are times when absolute certainty is ours, when experience corroborates what we are saying or implying; for instance, that Great Britain is an island, that Queen Anne is dead, and that there is an ocean off the west coast of Ireland.

Here it is a question of facts to which we may not often refer explicitly, but they support other facts on innumerable occasions without themselves being mentioned. But there are other beliefs which arise out of facts and themselves make such an impact on the mind that we exclaim, "On this or these the heavens and the earth depend." Once seen or understood, everything falls into shape, and we have before us a philosophy of life which can and must be lived. When we make moral judgments, we deal with particular problems which have an answer; in this they are distinct from the religious decision in faith. In faith it is not *an* answer, it is *the* answer which we have to give. It is a matter of life or death, and we can hold nothing back. It should, however, also be seen in terms of truth; it makes sense of life, it rests on grounds which the reason approves, and it is consistent and all-embracing. I said that it was more than a fact, for it is an interpretation. If a man were to approach the Gospels or the evidences for Christianity with as prejudiced a mind a white may have against the colored in Alabama, they will appear, as to the Gentile, a piece of folly. Nevertheless the evidence is there, and this is borne out by many a convert. Before his conversion, he does not see enough convincing evidence for him to make up his mind, but once he is converted, innumerable details become visible which he had missed before. A similar experience falls to everyone who comes to new appreciations and that is why, as a lead to grasp the nature of faith, it is useful to take examples from the arts and from books, where it takes time and goodwill to understand what the artist or the writer had in mind. The lover of Jane Austen or of Melville or Hegel or Wittgenstein will know what I mean. Indeed those who criticize the analytic or linguistic philosophers are always being told that they lack understanding. In other words, we have to assimilate ourselves to artists and thinkers and become like-minded with them. God is the Logos and an artist in the sense that he has composed a supreme work of intellectual artistry. The composition is there for all to see; it consists of the Word made flesh and the words which tell mankind how to live and what there is to live for. Once too we have convinced ourselves that the story in the Gospels is basically true, we have to consider the chief figure in the story, his claims and his behavior, and their relevance to ourselves. If Christ be truly divine and if his message be also of a divine quality, to understand it we shall need to have something approaching a divine understanding ourselves; for no matter how we try, we cannot reckon that we can have the same mind as God. And yet—this is just what Christianity means by faith, that by grace we do have the mind of Christ and begin the unending story of life with and in Him. We "put on" Christ; we wear his mask and impersonate him. Everything here is drawn together, or, what comes to the same thing, in following the Christ, we discover the way and the way is the way of truth, and it is in the way of truth that a philosophy of life can be lived.

The panorama opened by faith is, in short, this: a living God creating all but, in particular, man out of love, so as to get the best out of man and crown him with supreme happiness. This stands out by contrast with an immense dead universe to which we can assign neither beginning nor end, and human beings, like phosphorescent flies, flitting about in it. Such a cold picture is hardly to be borne; so all manner of idols have been set up, abstract absolutes and wholes, progress and humanity to make do and pacify the inquiring and restless soul of man. Those who, in reaction against too human idols, turn to some power for good or a spiritual principle or Absolute Spirit or Superconsciousness are making declarations out of weakness; for the habit of thinking in abstractions and with the help of the impersonal is a congenital weakness of the human mind and not a strength. We must always get back to what is living and to what is indicated, however feebly, by our own rushlight of personality. "I come to give life and that more abundantly" should be on the doorway of all schools of philosophy; to turn our backs on what is living is suicide. The principle behind all must, therefore, be a living God. By the aforesaid weakness of the human mind, all the attributes we make to God sound abstract, and for brevity and convenience, we speak of God's Mercy and Omnipotence and Love. We know that they are there in God and that in fact they exist only because God, the very life which has to be described in these terms, is what He is. So long as we remember this, all is well, and it reminds us that, though the human mind can take cognizance of God, it loses itself immediately. It cannot sort out what these attributes are in their abstraction and how they are all compatible in one Being. We are saved from otiose speculation by the revelation of God's nature in the Gospels. Metaphysics is not taught us there, but we do learn by great images, such as that of Fatherhood, and by the assurance that we cannot go wrong if we think of God as Love. God then brings finite reality into being. I know not how, except that as nothing finite can be God, the word "creation" serves a purpose, contrasting as it does the nothingness of the creature man, the "tenant of nothingness," in Heidegger's description, "with the plenitude of God."

As already must be clear, the ever-pressing problem has been that of the individual and his relationship with God, and then, concomitantly, the place of man in the world in the light of the Christian scheme of Redemption. Paul Tillich attributes to Original Sin what he calls "the split between the created goodness of things and their distorted existence." Too metaphysical and abstract for some tastes, this statement does refer to a characteristic of human life which is unmistakable and heartbreaking. Reformers and prophets see their efforts ruined time and time again by the sheer perversity of those they wish to help. It is clear that far too often for safety human beings are at cross-purposes with themselves and those around them. Man not only makes enemies, he is at enmity with himself, Furthermore, it is worth noting that this alienation within the self is witness to a disorder within man's constitution, and some Christian writers look there for the chief evidence of an original human and spiritual catastrophe. Such a catastrophe is, however, more clearly branded in the almost diabolical hatred which some men show towards their fellows or in that satanic pride which is without any human compassion, but can by its very grandeur elicit fear and envy, as in Milton's Lucifer. The same effect, under another aspect of Original Sin, is that the love of self, namely Eros, swells into a vice; a man becomes ingrowing instead of outgrowing. *Agape* would take him outward and upward, but *Agape* is not there. Now it is this condition which is healed by the Redemption. By the loving act of God made man, we are translated out of this condition into divinity without losing our selfhood. All the mystery and glory lie here for it is easy to imagine remedies which remove the self in the very process of removing the stain, or leave the stain and just cover it up from sight. A living philosophy opens out for us when we see God as living and loving, and man finding reconciliation and blissful life in that love. Two texts bring this out. The first is Christ's word: "And I being lifted up will draw all things to myself." The second is in the First Letter of St. John where he says that truth attests "that God has given us eternal life, and this life is to be found in His Son." This being lifted up refers to the Cross, but it can be metaphorically extended to the truth that, through the Cross, we too are being lifted up into the new life. This process of being "lifted up" or transformed is the warp and woof of the Christian philosophy of history. Oscar Cullman explains history after the victory of Christ in his Resurrection as an "interim" time before the Second Coming. In this he underestimated the work which is being accomplished by the Redemption here and now and through the years A.D. God in Christ is treating every individual as a miniature cosmos and is winning the human self's acceptance of His transforming love. God is inviting him to find his true, though new, name and to throw away the masks which are artificial or of only temporary use and to "put on" Christ. But besides the secret *entretien* with the individual, there is also the divine and decisive act of Redemption recapitulated in every place and throughout time. What happened at a supper room in Jerusalem and on Golgotha is not a local event; it is to make itself real everywhere and for every person. It is the one divine public act, like to the central act of the religion of Israel, but now under the New Covenant. God has tabernacled among men, and His presence is both symbolized in the Eucharistic liturgy and realized in the changing of the Bread and Wine. Here in this mystery of faith, God's transforming power over the lives of men is dramatized in signs and symbols and in the timeless oblation of His flesh and blood.

As at the beginning, so we are told by anthropologists, the sacred and the secular were so mingled that it took time for them to be separated now, since the advent and sacrifice of the Son of Man, what had become more and more alien is once more being reconciled in time. Similarly as the individuals of a tribe enjoyed a kind of co-conscious existence, so a new co-conscious body is being formed of living members with Christ, its Head. The secular world of nature and men, though it may have secrets which will never be revealed until the end, has become better known with every generation, and, certainly, so far as nature is concerned, knowledge has grown by leaps and bounds in the last one hundred and fifty years. What new thing then could Christianity have to say about nature and man? Of man it can be said that a new idea of him is presented of which the implications are so vast as to baffle the mind. Each individual so grows in stature that he fills the universe, and it becomes difficult to make the Christian view fit the people we brush up against at the rush hour. "Man has a prejudice against himself," Santayana tells us, and in truth, we have not made the best of ourselves; but, still, the heights to which, according to the Christian faith, God has called us are a new revelation. Each person, as we have already seen, is unique and with a special function to perform in this life with the help of Providence. In the Christian dispensation, he has to "put on" Christ, and he has to do this both by preserving his selfhood and by belonging to what has been called the Mystical Body of Christ. Moreover, he has to do this while partaking in a world of activities, some of which seem far removed from any religious connotation. How then can both these objectives be attained, and how does nature and our interest in it serve the religious objective?

Now that almost every region of the earth has been explored and communication has been made comparatively simple, there is renewed hope of achieving a peaceful unity of the whole human race. The poet wrote of a unity "to which the whole creation moves." Christian teaching, though it has concentrated primarily, as it should, on the spiritual and religious unity of mankind through the Church, has, nevertheless, not been indifferent to the more general issue. How could it be, seeing that it holds that nature too falls within the Providential plan? Its demand that "seek ye first the kingdom of God and all things shall be added unto you" is not to be taken as meaning that the word "first" should be understood as "only." The Church has too much respect for human nature to neglect it. This, I say, though many preachers in the past and many spiritual works warn people against the dangers of preoccupation with the things of this world. What these preachers and writers have in mind is the common weakness of men and women, and they want to insist that first things should be put first. Human experience bears too frequent witness that we approve of what is better but follow what is worse. There seems, however, to be a special doctrine in Catholic teaching which helps us to see the place of human nature in our sanctification. In the Letters of St. Paul, there is a distinction which can be summed up in two words, "inhabitation" and "incorporation." Commonly theologians have treated them as synonymous. We are being transformed so as to share the divine nature and have a new name. This work we cannot do ourselves, for our best would only make us more attractively human; it is, therefore, the power of God's love which is responsible for the metamorphosis. More technically, the theologians, on the strength of certain texts in St. Paul, attribute this work of our deification to the Holy Spirit, who dwells in us: "You are the temple of the Holy Spirit." Inhabitation is the correct technical word for this but, as I have said, often the word "incorporation" is used. It would be better if this word were reserved for another operation which is clearly intended by God in our regard. The words "Mystical Body" have already been used to signify the mode in which Christ, after his Resurrection, has covenanted to achieve his design of making us all one in Him. "All one in Him" has in the Christian dispensation a more precise meaning. The Son of God worked our redemption in and through his human nature which he had assumed. In the years of his life before his death and Resurrection, he belonged to one race; he spoke Aramaic and he passed all his grown-up life in a tiny province of the Roman Empire. But in his new, risen life, he throws off all these limitations; he is still the Christ, who was born of the Virgin Mary and suffered under Pontius Pilate, but he is also now the cosmic Christ, with his human nature expressing unchecked his divinity, and he chose, as the ceremony at the Last Supper shows, to join all mankind to himself through his own body and blood. The New Covenant is more realistic even than the premonitory act when the lintels of Jews were smeared with blood to save them from death and destruction. So profoundly convinced were St. Paul and St. John that this was the intention of Christ that they multiply images such as that of the head of a body and its members or a vine and its branches or marriage or rebirth, to show how living and real and even corporeal the new relation set up between Christ and those who believe in him is to be. St. Paul writes of filling up what is wanting to the sufferings of Christ, of the stature of Christ growing, and of our being recognizable as no longer our former selves, but as Christ. Now the word "incorporation" comports all this, and it is in the light of this doctrine that we are to understand what is meant by our having a new name, of being transformed and of our finding ourselves anew in the divine *Agape*.

By this interpretation of "incorporation," we are brought to see a close connection between our new life in Christ, and our human nature, and nature itself, closer in fact, than has been hitherto assumed. Already the argument of Barth and some Catholic theologians that human values are a waste product has been rejected. Our life in Christ is to be consummated by the resurrection of the body, and therefore all that we experience in this life can be revived again, transposed into a new key, and orchestrated into a larger theme. What perhaps may cause perplexity is how to conceive of a risen body. C.S. Lewis has pointed out how we can make do with one sense what really belongs to the five, each with its particular function. Going a step further, we can appeal to what is called the "phantom leg" experience. It is well known that patients who have had a leg cut off can nevertheless experience feelings and pain in what is no longer there, and that for a considerable time. Other odd experiences should be quoted: of how the body can make up for the loss of an eye or an arm by concentrating double power in the remaining eye or arm, or, still more interesting and relevant, how, as the resources of the senses are less than those of the emotions, the senses compensate by using the same sensation to express more than one emotion. This power of substitution and transposition provides a clue to the way in which an earthly experience can be doubled or recognized in a higher condition of life. Other apposite examples of this are at hand: a prose piece or poem composed in a rich language with a large vocabulary can be adequately translated into a poor language where words have to have several senses; or, still better, music composed for an orchestra can be transferred to a piano. So, too, concludes Lewis, our humanity can, while still remaining itself, be transposed into a divine mode.

Jean Guitton says that the manner a human being develops from embryo to death itself displays a rhythm of self-renewal. At first the embryo, as it is grafted and nourished in the womb of another's body, performs the movements which are needed to get itself freed in birth. Here is the first phase, and at the end of it, the primitive symbiosis is broken. Its conclusion spells the beginning of individual freedom and selfhood. The independence, however, is at first little more than in name, for the baby is helpless and depends on others for food, for significant speech, and for other characteristics, such as race. As the years pass, these first necessities pass away, and a new freedom is acquired at puberty, and again at the time when the human being is said to be grown-up. From then on, new developments ensue: the spirit is more fully aware of the conflicts of sex and purity within itself; it becomes conscious of its encounters with others and of its place in society. This phase can be said to end with marriage, companionship, and a career freely chosen. Where there is normal health and goodwill, body and spirit grow harmonious, and, instead of proving an obstacle, the body assists the movements of the spirit, abetting it in its pursuit of ideals and liberties beyond its present condition and scope. In this way the body prepares and disciplines the spirit for another new birth, death, when in a last great option the self will pass from a chrysalis stage to a new selfhood, to be co-conscious in the divinized humanity of Christ.

Guitton is in no doubt that a higher form of love is disclosed in human marriage. So far from the libido dominating all our idealism, or the body being an impediment of spiritual love, as some followers of Freud think, he uses this very libido as an accomplice in his defense of the spirit. At first he says he found something scandalous in the intimate association of pure love with the mechanism of reproduction. However, on closer inspection, a certain congruity shows itself between sex and spiritual love. So far from the human condition, as it is now, being accidental, it is as if some presiding genius were watching over the expression of love and regulating the human lottery. Sex shows itself as the surest means of arousing and sustaining love. On the one hand the permanence of the human species is assured, and on the other, the greater variety of the individual procured. The vital energies lead on to their transformation into something spiritual. What was originally carnality ends in being heavenly; the mere bodily function of animal breeding acquires an intrinsic value of its own, so that love takes a higher place even than knowledge in the scale of human excellence. This cooperation of the body with what is above it is not haphazard. Far from it: for it is an observable fact that the highest spiritual experiences fall to those who are faithful to the institutes of nature. Hence Guitton concludes that the art of loving is not in the least what the libertine tradition would have us believe. It is rather the art and science of making the fleeting loves of youth endure and multiply in fresh waves of experience throughout the course of a long human life. Love is no episode; it imposes itself like a divinity, regulating and inspiring and offering the promises of an undreamed of perfection. Such a perfection is not a *deus ex machina*; it emerges from the temporal experiences of our daily human life. It is the harbinger of what is to come, the larval state preceding the metamorphosis at death into a new life, which will contain all that is best in our former state.

Earlier Christian thinkers, relying on Plato and Aristotle, attempted to work out a complete statement of man's moral nature; his duties and desires, commandments and ideals. They were concerned to show that certain acts were unnatural and wrong, and that man had an end for which to live, even though this end could be made more wonderful by his love of another, especially if that other were God.

More attention to the nature of love has been given by the Catholic philosophers in recent years. One of the first to start the probing into it was Maurice Blondel in his book *L'Action*. He ended this work by saying that one had to make an option: no human ideal satisfied, it merely impelled one on to further loves; so that finally one had to choose either to pursue love endlessly or go down on one's knees and ask for infinite love. Blondel found inspiration in St. Augustine, and in his treatise on blessedness Aquinas had made use of a distinction made by Augustine between evening and morning knowledge. The evening knowledge includes most forms of imperfect happiness. Augustine says that evening knowledge comes from self-regard, and morning knowledge comes when the soul turns itself to God. In the first kind, God is known in the mind or self which knows; in the second, the mind or self knows itself better in God. The first is inferior and egocentric; the second is all for God and through *Agape*. St. Thomas, however, in referring to the second, is concerned with distinguishing the joy which comes in the vision of God Himself from the joys which accompany it, such as the enjoyment of friends. For the rest St. Thomas is echoing Aristotle. Happiness, he says, can be perfect or imperfect, natural or supernatural. By the imperfect is understood the degree of temporal or earthly happiness which man can attain; perfect happiness belongs to the celestial and everlasting.

The clue to the proper answer is, I believe, in the Augustinian distinction between the evening and morning loves, and if that sounds too poetical, between *Eros* and *Agape*. *Eros*, we have seen, in man is the expression of the possesive and self-realizing activity of man, whereas *Agape* always implies the desire to belong to another and to exist in his or her love. It is our own nature which cries out to us that it must not only survive but grow, taking into its own life all that is suitable; self-realization, self-interest, self-perfection are descriptive of the processes of any living thing, animal or spiritual, and in man this process is predominantly in the mind which craves to know and master facts and possess wisdom and enjoy God. Now along this line there is indefinite progress. Its criterion for what is good or bad morally is whether or not the act tends towards the welfare of our nature or not. It has directives; it lives "according to right reason"; it puts spirit above body and it abominates the misuse of a human function. If man had nothing else to boast about, he would always be ultimately self-centered. He has, however, another love which takes him outside himself, which philosophically can be traced back to man's dependent existence, just as *Eros* can be traced back to nature or essence. It is this *Agape* which stretches out in suppliant love to God, and it is this love which is the key to the self and its relation with God. Human beings do not stop at their own nature or their own perfection; they have not got one. From the beginning God has intended to transpose human nature to a higher scale or pitch; and this is why fundamentally man does not know who he is and why it is necessary that he should wear a mask and impersonate divinity. Life on earth and all its temporal phases are our unfinished condition, as unfinished as that of a grub or a chrysalis; and the grub could make many wrong guesses as to its proper name.

There remains the question as to how nature participates in the reconciliation of all things in Christ. The justification for meditating on this obscure and mysterious subject is St. Paul's definite assurance that nature is not to be left out. St. John has told us that there is to be a "new heaven and a new earth," but this might have been taken for special apocalyptic language were it not that St. Paul tells us that "nature in its turn will be set free from the tyranny of corruption, to share in the glorious freedom of the sons of God." This is to come about because of "God's loving design, centered in Christ, to give history its fulfillment by resuming everything in Him, all that is in heaven, all that is on earth, summed up in Him." By bringing together the hypothesis of evolution and the doctrine of the transformation of man into Christ in his Mystical Body, P. Teilhard de Chardin has daringly tried to offer an explanation of the role of nature. He is, I think, the first Catholic philosopher and scientist to make capital out of the theory of evolution. There have been many distinguished clerics who have brought religious faith and science together, men like Abbé Mendel and Abbé Breuil, but they were content to cultivate their own garden and not embroil themselves in general questions. Before Darwin, Christian philosophy, in company with the generality of philosophers, had regarded the world as an unmoving immensity, which had to be exploited or enjoyed, but few saw its relevance to the spiritual problems of man's ascent to God. It was generally looked upon as a place to be passed through in one's pilgrim's progress. Hegel was among the first to look upon creation as on the move. But as Hegel implied that God too was on the move and bound up with the dialectic of history, orthodox Christianity did not feel that it had anything to learn from him. Unfortunately too, partly through the fault of the Christian apologists of the time, evolution was taken under the wing of opponents of Christianity and religion. However, P. Teilhard de Chardin saw the connection between the metamorphosis of man and the world evolving around him. If nature itself progresses, and man himself, looked at from the scientist's point of view, is an emergent phenomenon of nature, may not the two, despite their differences, have a common destiny in the eyes of God? He hazarded a theory how this might be. In briefest terms, it was this: In nature, growing complexity reaches a stage where the combinations show signs of what is called life, life in its lowest forms. Then, with developing complexity again, the primitive forms develop through plant life and animal life, until finally man emerges. With the coming of man, however, the process goes on, but it also reverses itself; for while there is still increasing complexity of structure, man has a singular prerogative, namely, the power of rational reflection. That means that there is no longer just a developing physical progress; it is being reflected and understood for what it is, and in a mind. The mind can go back upon the whole past of evolution and trace out its steps, and find its significance. This gives to man a kind of sovereignty in nature, and as men keep on thinking, there comes nearer and nearer the possibility that the truth about the nature of the universe can be found, and when found, be enjoyed by all men thinking in unison. Truth, however, is not sufficient; there is need also at one and co-consciously aware of truth, and so at peace that they could be called in their unity almost a new species. Here would be a new and higher form of symbiosis where mankind has only one way of looking and seeing and one heart. Such an ideal, however, and such finality presuppose a presiding power or Providence, an of concord and love. So the dream may come true, and it looks as if the whole purpose of the evolving universe was towards this very end, that a universal society should be Alpha, who stands at the beginning, who is the Logos, the word who gives order and intelligibility to the evolutionary trend, guiding it in its ever-increasing complexity and perfection and summing it all up at the end, Alpha and Omega. This new species, too, cannot exist save with a center of life to it, and this is the cosmic Christ, who gathers mortals into an organic superaggregation of souls. With this culmination, "mankind has succeeded, not only in becoming cosmopolitan, but in stretching a single organized membrane over the earth without breaking it."

One critic describes the function of Omega as follows: "The universe itself is informed with psychic energy and somewhere on a line which passes through the axis of all possible universes is Point Omega, at the center, as it were, of the whole space-time continuum from which pours out the spiritual force and radiance which certain mystics and saints can dimly comprehend. The goal of evolution is that all should comprehend, and that finally humanity should open its parachute and perform an act of psychic union with Point Omega. . . ." Many have disagreed with this vision and prophetical interpretation of reality; scientists, philosophers, and theologians all being captious about what touches on their own field. It is better, I think, to see it as blazing a new trail and, as such, deserving of the highest praise, than as a finished study. For this reason I do not put it forward except as providing the open sesame to others who wish for a livable philosophy in which the discoveries of science can be incorporated. Perhaps we are not yet ready to do more than give a tentative and preliminary sketch of the ways of God in relation both to nature and to man. Scientists are at the moment in a skeptical mood about the nature of their results and their bearing on ultimate reality. Historians, too, to judge from their reactions to the world of Spengler and Toynbee, do not at the moment care overmuch for philosophies of history. We are nevertheless encouraged to look to a total reorientation of the world as well as of man to its Head Christ in the writings of St. Paul. "All things," he tells us, "are to be restored in Christ"; and that this is no mere loving superlative is proved by numerous other texts which show that a very definite idea was in St. Paul's mind. Christ is "to dominate over all things, visible and invisible, which the Father has conferred upon Him." "He (Christ) will form this humbled body of ours anew, molding it into the image of His glorified body; so effective is His power to make all things obey Him"; for it is God's "loving design, centered in Christ, to give history its fulfillment by resuming everything in Him, all that is in heaven, all that is on earth, summed up in Him"; and then at the end of history, Christ "will surrender the kingdom to God the Father." It is natural, therefore, for Teilhard de Chardin to see Christ as the link between science and history. The way in which man is admitted under the headship of Christ is by assimilation and impersonation; the "old man" dies in the symbolic action of water being poured over his head; he takes a new name when in the Eucharist, as in marriage, he is made one flesh and one spirit in Christ.

VIII

CREDO'S MAGNA CARTA

At the beginning I made a distinction between the certain and the true. By the certain I meant all those realities of everyday life, without which life would be just one long muddle and misunderstanding. Daily life is full of certainties stretching from the most banal home details to physics and chemistry, history and morals. But the more we move amongst the learned and so-called wise, the more will we be struck by the incompatibility of what they tell us about the universe, its nature and import, with these certainties which both they and we hold. One man is horrified by some act of selfishness or cruelty, though the night before, just before bedtime, he said that he believed that all morals were explicable in Freudian terms and that he was a materialist. Another will be very sensitive to criticism of his decisions and conduct, though in the lecture room he is a determinist and denies free will. Such examples of apparent inconsistency between daily certainties and a general philosophy, between the certain and the true, could be multiplied.

All of us look for a consistent view of life, not for the sake of consistency, but because the mind of its nature tries to make sense of what goes on within and without.

I take for granted that whatever station of life I am in it makes sense and fits in with some general order in the world. We quote proverbs and are not afraid to make some generalizations ourselves. No one really believes that moral good is just as subjective as a taste for beer in preference to stout or dry instead of sweet wine. Moral good is not like a chance wildflower picked up on a highway; it is the highway itself, the direction leading on to man's happiness and perfection. Just as in a play I expect to find a consistency in the actions, in succeeding scenes, and in the general plot, so I demand of governments and of historians that they should have some principles and ideals which guide their work. Throughout history, men and women have had opinions and beliefs about themselves and what they should do, even though the beliefs have been various and in conflict with one another.

We, then, take up attitudes to life and interpret what is going on around us in our own way. Naturally most of us would be shy of calling our attitude a philosophy; it sounds too highfalutin. But in fact it is a miniature philosophy, even if it be not worked up into what goes by the name of philosophy. "Wisdom is never silent; . . . There she stands, on some high vantage point by the public way, where the roads meet, or at the city's approach, close beside the gates, making proclamation." To some, the pursuit of this wisdom has meant everything and the passages in the Books of Proverbs and Wisdom have struck a responsive chord. It brings a yield better than gold or jewels, and therefore they have listened to it, believing that "the man who wins me, wins life, drinks deep of the Lord's favor; who fails, fails at his own bitter cost; to be my enemy is to be in love with death."

Kierkegaard in his own way sought such a kind of wisdom: "Let the understanding condemn what is transitory, let it clear the ground, then wonder comes in in the right place, the ground that is cleared in the changed man."

My first intention was to make a comparison between the Credo contained in the Christian message and other philosophies of life. But the difficulty of being fair to them and, at the same time, being short is too great. There are many views of life which are attractive and have been enticingly portrayed. In the ancient world there are the forms of Hindu and Buddhist religion, of which Zen, perhaps, is the best known in the West. Their weakness is that in neither is the divine principle made clearly loving and personal, nor is selfhood sufficiently safeguarded. Greece and Rome gave us Epicureanism and Stoicism, which, under varying names, have reappeared in history; the one identifying happiness and pleasure, the other clinging to stern duty. The Bloomsbury circle leaned towards the former in its fondness for high thinking and the love of friends. The most delicate shape of private living I know was delineated for me by H.B. Brewster in his book *The Prison*. There is no abiding unity to be found in this life, "only," he writes, "the futile effort to collect into an hour of consciousness the infinite and conflicting aspects of reality." Thoughts and explanations are too artificial; their "stiff, ungainly fingers only desecrate the sacred revelations which steal upon us and take us unawares." So he falls back on a kind of passivity or stillness, and then something overwhelms and stuns him and is mighty enough to break away from him. "If I seek to retain it and mingle it again with my substance by egress from which it was divine, it forthwith loses its divinity. . . . We are full of immortality. But it dwells not in the beauty of our moral person; it stirs and glitters in us under the crust of self, like a gleam of sirens under the ice, and any blow which breaks this crust brings us into the company of the eternal ones whom to feel is to be they."

This account is interesting in its rejections as well as in itself. Brewster sees that the active life is too full of accidents and uncertainties to be taken as ideal; it brings no interior contentment. Nor do any of those constructions or systems for which we are responsible fill us with a lasting satisfaction. We grow tired with our own thoughts and with those of our grandparents, however sublime. But Brewster himself has no brief to argue when he has to face suffering and the general acidity of life. How artificial his peace appears, when we think of Dachau or Ravensburg. There are only a few in privileged circumstances who could share Brewster's experience. Far more, I should think, who have to struggle for their living and to look after a family, would say that they must make the best of the life which lies before them, and probably they would admire those who have the grit to go on amid difficulties, who remain cheerful and goodnatured and make themselves available to their friends when needed. A less soaring ambition, but a common one. Nevertheless, no less than the aesthete's or the scientist's ideal is it inadequate in view of the possibilities of the human soul and life's temptations, opportunities, and sufferings. But above all, it is because of the transitoriness of life that human ideals such as these just portrayed will not serve; they are palliatives rather than ideals. This is the burden of the Existentialist song, that we go on and never arrive; we fall down dead.

But I learned soon enough that if a philosophy be

worthy of its name then it must be one which can be lived, one which must find its meaning rooted in a notion of person. But no philosophy is authentic which disregards death. The Christian view, it may be objected, pays too much attention to death, though it must be admitted that something like a death instinct is in man and it is, in a curious way, a tributary of the love which I have called centrifugal. As such death is always active and no doubt has insinuated itself often into religion. But the Christian faith can make a counter claim, that it "gives life and that more abundantly," and it is the only interpretation or philosophy which faces reality and is as wide as the world itself. The *Day of the Lord* pervades all the other days of the week like a sacrament. If the more recent judgments of the anthropologists be right, primitive man did not look on the world as profane and assign a portion of it to God as sacred. On the contrary, all was sacred at first, and it was only as man grew more conscious of himself and his autonomy that he took over the world as his own. Strange to tell, we are being told now that once again the sacred must be sought in the secular, though the chief exponent of this idea did not mean what the primitives meant. That the sacred, as the Christian understands it, does like a rich tapestry include all that is called secular is the theme of the poet and painter David Jones. This theme is worked out in his *Anathemata* and explained in an essay in a composite work named *Catholic Approaches*. There is, he tells us, a unity in all art, as used in the sense of "making," despite the obvious dissimilarities of "a Diesel engine, bootmaking, English prose, radar, horticulture, carpentry, and the celebration of the Sacred Mysteries. There must be a common factor, for the 'desire and pursuit of the whole' is native to us all. In early days all making was a sacred activity, and as long as man continues to be a signmaker, sacredness cannot be absent from his work. His moral nature does not account for this, nor his speculative intelligence. Some philosophers have despised "signs' as indicating a defect in our human composition; our minds have to be prodded into activity by the sense and by sensible signs." But surely, argues David Jones, art is too striking a prerogative to be attributed to some infirmity of our human nature. Its great successes point to its having a special role; and that is to provide us with a sign or sacrament of the holy. "A man," he says, "cannot only smell roses . . . but he can, and does and ought to, pluck roses, and he can predicate of roses such and such. He can make a signum of roses. He can make attar of roses. He can garland them and make anathemata; which is presumably the kind of thing he is meant to do. . . . No wonder then that theology regards the body as a unique good. Without body; without sacrament. Angels only; no sacrament. Beasts only; no sacrament. Men; sacrament at every turn and all levels of the 'profane' and 'sacred' in the trivial and in the profound; no escape from sacrament." Christianity, above all other religions, has exploited this trait in man of using signs and sacraments. In his *Anathemata,* he compared the Eucharist to the life of a tree and how the rings in the trunk, as the centuries passed, revealed the interconnection of sacred and secular.

Concerning this concordance of the sacred and the secular, I wrote, in a book called *No Absent God,* that man ceases to know himself when he ceases to know God. The secular world is not self-sufficient, nor has any secular answer been able to breathe life into its dry bones. There is no fullness of being in this life so far, nor is there any prospect of it in the future. There is richness, but it goes astray unless it be worked into a philosophy which knows how to remedy the ravages of time and parry its death-dealing stroke. That is one reason why historians like Arnold Toynbee are attracted by the Christian answer. True, he has forsaken it in his latest work, but many see his most forcible argument reaching a conclusion at the end of his sixth volume. The artist David Jones sees images and analogies and presentiments everywhere of the great Christian mystery; Toynbee saw Christianity as the one force which supremely met the challenge of life. Other claimants he had examined and he had tested them, and in the end he saw them as falling by the wayside. "Company after company fell out of the race, the warrior heroes, those who lived in the past, and those who lived in the future; then the philosophers, until only the gods were left in the running. But even among them few dared to face the severest ordeals of life; and he straightway fills the whole horizon. There is the Saviour, and the pleasure of the Lord shall prosper in His hand; He shall see of the travail of His soul and shall be satisfied."

Here the test is not strictly intellectual, that of truth, a test which must come first; it is rather a pragmatic one, of what can bear up against all the crises of life, the successes and calamities of living, what, too, moves with undiminished light through history, ever gaining in size and glory, and therefore possessed of the fullness of life and the portfolio of immortality. Toynbee, writing history, has naturally in mind secular experience, and it is a fair test. Mr. Will Herberg, writing in *Encounter* for November 1963 does not seem so confident as Toynbee about the success of Christianity. He does not believe that we can judge Christianity on intellectual ground, nor, on the other hand, can speculative atheist philosophers who "claim to be able to refute arguments for God's existence" avail to destroy it. We cannot help taking up an attitude and this is our religion. Man is by nature a *homo religiosus,* and the real question is what kind of a god he worships and what form the religion takes. Herberg then goes on to say that the Christian religion has lost its premiership in modern civilization because it seemed to disbelieve in the possibilities of science and technology. It insulted man by disbelieving in him and his resources. Now, however, after the catastrophes of the twentieth century, a new religious and metaphysical vacuum is being created. The problem of our day is who shall fill it, a new Ersatz-religion or Christianity?

Herberg here is so nearly right that it is a pity he accepts unquestioningly the separation made by the school of existentialist theologians between "speculative" thought and "existential reality." (These are Herberg's words.) It will not ultimately do any good to the Christian religion or to any religion to hide it away from the inquisition of truth. It must satisfy the mind, and in fact the mind is a better test than the one proposed by Herberg. After all, the same kind of complaint as his against the Christian religion was made at the end of the Roman Empire, namely that it was out of touch with what was happening. Again in the last four hundred years, there have been philosophic and scientific theories which the Church was told to favor at peril of its life; they are dead and the Church may have scars but is undamaged. Kierkegaard and the Existentialists have given to us many new insights, and they have unbared the naked condition of the human spirit; they lived too and still live at a time when it was natural to exaggerate the shortcomings of speculative thinkers and to forsake the metaphysical approach. But by doing so, they have withdrawn from the pure stream of truth. At the moment, instead of a clear issue and of the reaction to the question of religion by the whole man, with his mind, emotions, and desires, we are led into a morass where muddied words, like commitment, existential predicament, ultimate concern are bandied about, and atheism and theism, religion and concern, sacred and secular are made to look almost alike. The immensely valuable insights of Kierkegaard and others are turned into ritual phrases. Not that the philosophers are without blame. Herberg is right in thinking that there is now a "religious and metaphysical vacuum," and the lack of a love of wisdom among the philosophers is partly responsible. Truth dangling all by itself is made into an object to be shot at or turned into a game.

Wisdom, as distinguished from knowledge, connotes a connection between thinking and loving; and one of the reasons why Existentialism appealed to so many was its emphasis on the importance of love and concern and personal choice. It is the self which has a mind and feels and is hurt, and all ultimately goes back to the problem of the self. It has to take up an attitude, to make its own interpretation of life, and yet never let the subjective interfere with objective truth. This has been the problem discussed throughout these pages. It is the mind which has the vision of the shape of the world and of man's place in it and man's relationship with God. Desire, stimulates the mind and makes it see what otherwise would pass unnoticed. "Faith too, has its own eyes," St. Augustine tells us; so that when it comes to the understanding of God's truth, when revealed, reason is blinded without the help of grace. But when I enter into a dialogue or dispute with another, be he theist or agnostic, I cannot take advantage of any superior grace or light, nor is there any need to do so. We all know those moments in the development of our thought when disparate themes come together and make a new unity; how we then are shaken out of our complacency and ask ourselves how we could have been so blind or so narrow before, but we cannot appeal to a critic of our new view to wait on the same flash of light or accept our authority for it; we must meet on the level of reason and let the truth appear. So it is that a Credo pronounced and accepted in youth can come to mean more and more, as confirmations flock in from experience and ideas reach towards a rounded whole. The interpretation remains all the while intellectual, but our beliefs come nearer and nearer to being a love story.

But how, it may be asked, can I expect a reader to believe that what I believed when I was a boy and a young priest can remain intact when I have so often left the cloister and traveled over the world? Have I been untouched utterly by the advances made in scholarship, in philosophy, in science? Has human experience left me and my beliefs completely immune? The problem has recently taken an acute form and been formulated by Rudolf Bultmann in his *Jesus Christ and Mythology*. In his view the Gospel story is an attempt to express the impression made by a historical figure, Jesus Christ, upon his followers. So deep and significant was that impression that it had to be expressed in the grandiose language, which came naturally to the Jews at the time. Hence all the events which describe the coming of a celestial being, the virgin birth, angels, miracles, resurrection, and ascension, must be treated as mythology. To get at the truth in the Gospels, we must demythologize them. This may sound easy, but in fact so much is left to the arbitrary assumptions of each critic that at the end the Gospels would cease to be living documents and the person described in them would be featureless. We have to suppose, too, that the evangelists were remarkably insouciant. What is more, we should have to face a miracle of a different kind. They are not always "grandiose" in their story of Christ: he does not follow the pattern of the saint or hero, for there are incidents which might shock readers, such as the agony in the Garden of Olives. The apostles and disciples also do not come off too well; they are not made a good advertisement of the new religion.

The whole question of mythologizing seems to need far more critical consideration and reflection. Let us grant that the writers of the New Testament lived in a prescientific age. That means that normally such writers would be more credulous about what they were unable to test by their ordinary experience. In this matter, the evangelists show a remarkable sobriety in comparison with the legends, stories, and apocryphal gospels which circulated round about the same time. Then there is the matter of imagery and mythology about which Bultmann and Dr. J. Robinson are disturbed. It is true that prescientific writers do convey what they think true by pictorial images and myths, as scholars would say happened in the story of Adam and Eve. Nowadays we distinguish more carefully between actual events, truths contained in these events, and a mythical or pictorial way of communicating the truth. But does this mean that much in the Gospels and in the Christian revelation must therefore be scrapped? Bultmann and Robinson argue that in the early credal formularies a three-decker universe is presupposed: Heaven, Earth, and Hell; that God dwells on high with His angels, makes the world in seven days, and is met on mountaintops. The same kind of language is used for the advent of Christ and his departure from this world to sit at the right hand of God.

Now such pictorial language can be, and probably is, a stumbling block to minds disciplined to a dry accuracy in scientific or logical methods* They do not notice that outside the laboratory or the lecture hall they use the same kind of language themselves in talking of a blue sky and setting sun. To arrive at any wise conclusion in these matters we have to make distinctions. But, when a critic says that Christians in early days believed in a three-decker universe, he should also add that they well knew the distinction between the spiritual and the material, and believed in a universe of order, harmony, and unity—and it was on these, not on the images, that their theology was based. There is no such thing as a language without metaphor and images. We are creatures of space and time, and all our concepts come to us clothed in sensible images. Metaphor is a good example of a new association of thought with image, and for a metaphor, there must be the compresence both of the object and the likeness, as

---

* That images can be childish and nevertheless of much service is proved by the success of the Freudian techniques. Freud writes as if the processes below the level of consciousness were personal; they push and block like persons in a crowd. In this way he creates a whole mythology of the unconscious. To the philosopher and the scientist the idea of a conscious unconscious is verbiage, but it serves as a working model. The tendency to personalize abstractions and qualities and processes is so constant even amongst serious thinkers that it can almost be excused, so long as we can make out what the writer or speaker is trying to convey.

when the poet first realized that "my love is like a red, red rose." After a while the imagery is lost in the object. Furthermore, besides these cases of fusion, there are symbols which we use without ever noticing their metaphorical character. This is the case with primordial symbols, such as right and left, high and low, thin and thick, white and black. Of this latter kind are many Christian symbols such as the Fatherhood of God, the height of virtue, the depths of sin. There is no reason to suppose that an ancient, any more than a modern man, would be likely to think of spatial and physical qualities when he read or spoke with such metaphors. All through time, man has with great cleverness maneuvered even highly subjective experience into the world of discourse and communication by multiplying images from all his senses. He is also expert at finding analogies, which help to give a common currency to truths, analogies which run through all the grades of being, the inanimate, the bodily, and the spiritual. One simple example is when we speak of the wings of a plane on the analogy of birds, and then draw angels with wings to signify their swiftness of thought and action. It is because of our familiarity with such analogies and their commutations and permutations that we can enjoy the images which cluster around the signs of the Zodiac, Dante's "Seven Starred Wain of High Heaven," and William Blake's "To Hold Infinity in the Palm of Your Hand and Eternity in an Hour."

Dr. Robinson and other exaggerate the harm done to Christian belief by the use of imagery, even ancient and out-of-date imagery. They are entitled, nevertheless, to grumble. The very beauty of the scenes sculptured on the facades of cathedrals and churches, in paintings over altars and in stained glass, could well persuade the simple that heaven and hell were like this. (Stephen Daedalus had to listen to a sermon on hell at school in which it was depicted as a place of horrid sights and smells and fire.) The defense of such imagery is easy in theory; it should always be accompanied with an explanation of the conceptual and spiritual reality of what is imaged. God, it must be shown, is not an overgrown human person, but a subsistent being infinitely perfect, omniscient, and all loving.

God has no place; He is everywhere, and heaven is not a locality in space, as we understand these terms. Lastly there is an agony, the greatest a human being can suffer, which consists in the loss of God's love and consequent bitter loneliness. It was to save mankind from such a possible fate that God redeemed man, not by bargaining or buying back, but by identifying Himself with us, taking our name, and becoming the head of a new race. It is this mysterious love-act which is shadowed forth in the sacrificial rites of tribes and peoples. If this be once grasped, then it can be understood how time and again members of the Christian religion have almost caricatured the truth and, by their overdevotion and obstinate clinging to images and icons, led to the kind of protests we have just quoted. It might then be wise, in a world which is so apt to look upon ancient and medieval man as credulous and unscientific, to remove some of its more antique furniture and replace it with what is modern and acceptable. That would require a new investigation into which are now the favorite images and a glance at new expressions in our daily languages, expressions drawn from scientific devices, examples of speed and of distance overcome, depth psychology and new modes of communication. A genius might even write a new Apocalypse, abounding in images which could replace the walls of the city set with precious stones and the trumpets and incense and the angel with a cloud for a vesture.

Let images abound because the truths which they present are not essentially affected by time. Call "love" what one may, it remains the same. New aspects and depths can, however, be unendingly discovered, so that what is old can be made to look fresh to every new generation, and it can be enriched by the new discoveries and insights of humanity as it progresses in time. The man of 2000 A.D. will live by the same truths as the authors of the New Testament, Augustine, Aquinas, Copernicus, and the Abbé Mendel, but he will see them revarnished, with a patina of time and in new settings which reflect their truth. The early Christians started with what their contemporaries considered a fatal handicap. Their ideas were not contemporary; they sounded uncultured especially when expounded by obscure provincials in a kind of argot. St. Paul, when he spoke at the Areopagus was laughed out of the assembly, and his later admission that what he taught was to the Jews a stumbling block and to the Gentiles folly did not promise well for the success of Christianity. Celsus, one of the intellectual opponents of the new cult, accused it of frivolous novelty and of upsetting the great tradition which had made the Greco-Roman civilization the envy of the world. In Hellenistic circles, it seemed nonsense to mix the divine and the human, the unchanging and necessary with what was changeable and therefore radically imperfect and half unreal. That time could be important to the gods, and that God could enter time belonged to the world of fancy and fairy tale.

Faced with such resistances, racial, intellectual, and

religious, there did not seem much hope for the Christian religion. Like other mystery religions, it might touch the effervescent strain in human nature, excite the populace, especially women, have its say, and then die out. Its growth, however, showed that it had a universal appeal as well as a special quality in the person of its founder. As a form of worship, it gathered up the rituals and liturgies preceding it and transformed them into a unique, sacramental meal and sacrifice, which both symbolized and acted out the most intimate love-relationship between God and man. Intellectually, the coming of the Lord explained the riddling syncretistic philosophies, and a new personal theology developed which brought a new hope to man in his predicament. Furthermore, by its human traits, its defense of the body against the Gnostics, its acceptance of the physical world and the splendor of human nature against the Manichees, it gave the magna carta, a freedom of entrance, to all genuine human experience, scientific, philosophical, artistic, and religious. At moments its officials and members have shown themselves obscurantist and unworthy of their commission. It has been very human as well as divine. "It has learned the secrets of the grave, has been a diver in deep seas of thought, and trafficked for strange cargoes. Yet all this has been to it but as the sound of lyres and flutes, and lives only in the delicacy with which it has molded its changing lineaments and features." A purple passage from another writer puts in short what perhaps could not else be said, how the Greek and Roman influence passed through the Church's hands and mingled with that of a colder clime and flashed out in the Norman splendor in Rheims and Palermo and the kingdom of Jerusalem. "And yet an auguster thing than Aristotle or Harmodius and

Aristogeiton held the framework together; the faith, which drew all the trials and the experiences and the love into a new life. All was swept into this kingdom, race and royalty and right divine; the village headman's rules of custom, the camel-hair tents and horses of the Ukraine; the red sailing ships of the Normans to the mosque of Cordova, boarding the Santa Marias in quest of new worlds richer than Cathay; lighting the torch of learning at Bologna, Padua, Paris, and Oxford, and building great works of mercy for the poor and infirm and making women the ideal of chivalry." The last few centuries have not been so illustrative of its transforming power, except in far pagan lands, because the arts and sciences had come of age and therefore relied on their own postulates and resources. But in the social life of the West, the gradual emergence of the principles of liberty, equality, and fraternity witness to its silent strength. Men and women are not equal physically or in their gifts, but only on the spiritual idea that they are all images of God. Hence, basically, people of today with their sensitiveness to freedom are living on the message of St. Paul to Philemon, whose young slave Onesimus, had taken refuge with Paul: "Think of him no longer as a slave; he is something more than a slave, a well-loved brother, to me in a special way; much more, then to thee, now that both nature and Christ make him thy own."

Nowadays even the possibility of a Credo has to be vindicated. The possibility is there because of the power we have of interpreting phenomena, of grasping constellations of events, of enlarging the whole, and finally arriving at what is universal enough to be called a philosophy of life. We have to make sense of life, and we have to have a philosophy which we can live. The differentiating mark of a Christian philosophy or Credo is that it holds that there is a God, that there is such an intimate relation of God to the self that the self withers in God's absence; next, that God, out of love, has entered history and established a still closer relationship by reconciling man to himself and making him a sharer in the divine nature. This happens without any diminution of selfhood and the possibilities of human nature; on the contrary, God comes "to give life and that more abundantly." This divinization of man involves a metamorphosis or transformation of man—and it is at this point that Christianity makes its departure from other philosophies, even theistic ones. That this is new is, I think, shown by the scare caused even amongst good and intelligent people by Teilhard de Chardin's suggestion that man was moving to a new and higher species. I do not believe, so long as man is upon this earth, that he will evolve into a new species, and even in the final dénouement of man in the kingdom of God, he will remain distinguishably human, however transformed. But such a transformation will come about, or rather, it is now and in time invisibly taking place; man is in a larval stage now, like mollusks, crustaceans, and certain amphibia. Amphibian is a choice word for what is happening to human nature through the gracious intentions of a loving God. Amphibian conveys the idea of belonging to two elements—and man is human and divinisable in the life of Christ; he is undergoing a metamorphosis. He has also a double activity, one masculine and centripetal, the other, feminine and centrifugal. The first maintains all that is human; the second moves out of self to loving sacrifice and union with the Godhead. Now since it is God's primary intention that all should enjoy this life with Him, we can say that it is God's intention actually now in operation for the whole human race.

It follows from this that human beings are as much in search of themselves as they are of other desirable objects, and the common desire for a good name and reputation, for monuments which record their good deeds, derive from this fundamental search. Original sin, according to Catholic doctrine, has obscured the knowledge of ourselves by producing conflict within us; but apart from this, as we are in a phase of change, we are easily confused as to our identity, especially, when corroborating voices and an informative philosophy are absent. The grub and the amphibian reach their final stages by natural processes; not so with man, who grows by means of assimilation and impersonation, that is, by "putting on" a character or persona or mask. We cannot help putting on masks, and the danger is that we put on the wrong mask and identify ourselves with what we are not and what we should not be. The philosophies we have examined in these pages bear this out, for they tell us that we are in a state of *ek-stase,* outside ourselves and feeling our way to being, *pour sois* who want to be rid of the condition they are in; they work to be prospective owners of their lives instead of being mere lessees. The Christian religion acknowledges that there is some truth in this Existentialist complaint and says that this life is the period of transformation, and that in the next life we shall have an authentic self and that this final self we shall discover in God's loving regard and recognition of us.

This philosophy does not, therefore, put the be-all and end-all in this life, and in this it departs, as I have said, from most other philosophies of man. They expect to find out all about him now; they also expect to understand fully what the moral order consists of. The Christian, on the other hand, sees this as the prelude or larval stage which contains the promise of what is to come. That is why faith is described in the Letter to the Hebrews as "the substance of things hoped for, the evidence of things unseen." Oscar Cullmann goes with us up to a point; he realizes that the redemptive act of Christ is so decisive as to end history. But when he calls the period we live in a kind of aftermath or "interim," he underestimates the importance of the act of Christ who is in the world still and re-forming man to the likeness of himself. Instead, then, of this being called an "interim" time, its name should be "the phase of the Lord, the *transitus Domini,*" and the full meaning of the letters A.D. should be properly appreciated.

From another angle, we can see that the Christian view of death is radically different from that of the Existentialists. As the Existentialists have exposed a native and perpetual condition of human life, it would seem as if the Christian view diverges from the majority, if not all, of contemporary and past philosophies. Death is the sword in all human aspirations. Many feel that death makes all life meaningless, for we are never certain that any good work will be completed or, if completed, last. Nature seems indifferent to whether it be the good or the bad deed which is interred. Once gone, too, there is no return. It is for these and other reasons that so many philosophers insist that "Angst" and "concern" are the most revealing and representative of all our emotions; they hint that men and women build themselves temporary shelters, or retreats, where they can forget what is to come, or behave, after the manner of Christian Scientists towards pain and death, as if they were unreal.

From the very first Christianity taught that death had lost its sting: "O death, where is thy sting; O death, where is thy victory." Death is saluted as the birthday into the new life. Seen in this way, not only death, but suffering, physical and spiritual, also ceases to be unbearable. If death ends all, then a stoic resignation is all that can be expected, but in the knowledge of an eternity of joy to come, pain is bearable. Still more is this true when it ceases to be meaningless. Now such is the solidarity of the human race, and again of family and community groups, that each person shares the joys and sufferings of the others. There is an Arab legend to the effect that there are always in the world thirty princes who carry the world on their shoulders and rescue it. In the Christian dispensation no man is an island; his good acts are so graced as to bring relief to others in distress, physical or spiritual. It is on this principle that beings who are barely human, like the Southern Kurelu, Stone Age savages in the Central Highlands of New Guinea, thrive and show the likeness to God in them in the love radiating out from the members of Christ's Body. Warmed by a spiritual sun, they are made ready for transformation into the Kingdom of God. So it is that in facing the worst a philosophy of hope emerges, one which does not shut its eyes to death and suffering and evil, but sees in them, wherever a speck of goodwill exists, the gateway to resurrection and a higher order of life. This heavenly life has often been represented as a complete break with life on earth; first a time of struggle and temptation, and then the reward, the translation to a better life. But there is a close connection between the two forms of life, and it is not a question of translation so much as of transformation. The impersonation is finished at death and the new unique portrait of Christ is completed, and Christ in his recapitulation of all things in himself, has, please God, at our death fulfilled himself in one more way. The mask is the clue to this, and with a legitimate exaggeration, we can say that the whole world has been wearing a mask, preparing to change it. St. Paul told his Corinthians that the "fashion of this world is passing." The Greek word is "schema," the present scenery and show, as in the old pantomimes all would end in a transformation scene. This was the great insight of Teilhard de Chardin, that evolution, the advance of nature, threw a light upon the ultimate restoration of all things in Christ. For centuries we have taken the image of leaving this earth over-seriously. We are to leave all behind and share in the spiritual joys of the Kingdom of God. But instead of our going up to Heaven, St. John writes of the heavenly city coming down to us. That is to say that "all things are made new": God "is all in all," and we and all else too are glorified in His love.

IX

EPILOGUE

By outlining and developing a religious Credo in such a philosophical and theological way, some may complain that I have left out "the one thing necessary" in religion, namely, personal experience. Such a criticism would not apply to a Behaviorist, and even a follower of Freud would not need to go beyond a scientific account of the subconscious. Assuredly every Christian has to be concerned primarily with loving God and loving his neighbor. This is the great commandment. But only a saint or a great sinner on his way to becoming a saint can without self-consciousness describe his or her interior life. There are great works showing the steps to be taken in the dark night of the soul, steps which experience has shown must be taken with the greatest prudence and humility. They vary much, as those who have looked at St. Francis de Sales's *Treatise on the Love of God, The Exercises of St. Ignatius,* or Augustine Baker's work *Santa Sophia* will know. One of my own favorites is the exquisitely beautiful and simple *Revelations of Divine Love* by Juliana of Norwich.

I do not hesitate to declare that man without an interior,

spiritual life is an empty husk. That does not mean that everyone needs to be introspective or to reflect much upon themselves. There are countless thousands who, from their outward behavior or their language, might be thought to ignore the life of the spirit, but I expect impressions are fallacious, as diaries sometimes show. Few would deny that there are multitudes of inarticulate, straightforward persons to be found in factories and on ships and on the land who put into practice the commandments and counsels of the Gospels. Many such as these are chosen in the Parables as being loved by God and the first to gain entrance to the Kingdom of God. With these should be joined the hard hit and all those mentioned in the Beatitudes. We are back, then, to a philosophy of life, a Credo, which must be lived. Whether we like it or not, the world is not one in which we can take our ease. As children, we used to be told how at the very moment that we were listening large numbers were being born, others dying, and many in great pain as well as joy. Their world must not be out of joint with ours, a Lazarus starving and covered with sores while we feast. The idea, as we have seen, is that we should be co-consciously one, and nothing shows more strikingly the greatness of St. Paul's heart than the words: "Who is hurt, and I am not hurt? Who is disappointed, and I am not disappointed?" The man who could write such words had a heart like that of God Himself in the width of its sympathy with and affection for others. They remind me of a friend of mine, now dead. On the mantelpiece of his room stood a small drawing of a hideously ugly man, with slit eyes and hardly any chin, and that unshaven. He was wearing a rough cap and scarf and ill-dressed. The title of the drawing was *The Hooligan*. Underneath it my friend had written the following lines from John Langland, the medieval poet, lines spoken in the poem by Christ:

> "Thy place is biggyd (built) above the starres clere;
> None other palace built in so stately wyse.
> Come on, my friend, my brother most entere,
> For thee I offryd up my blood in sacryfyse."